Journey X

Take Jesus from your Head to your Heart
Take your Religion to Relationship
Turn your Works into Worship

Gayle Nuckowski

Copyright © 2016 Celebrity Expert Author
All rights reserved. Unauthorized duplication or distribution is strictly prohibited.

ISBN-13: 978-0-9970968-7-3

ISBN-10: 0-9970968-7-X

Published by: Celebrity Expert Author
http://celebrityexpertauthor.com

Canadian Address:
501- 1155 The High Street,
Coquitlam, BC, Canada
V3B.7W4
Phone: (604) 941-3041
Fax: (604) 944-7993

US Address:
1300 Boblett Street
Unit A-218
Blaine, WA 98230
Phone: (866) 492-6623
Fax: (250) 493-6603

Note: The views expressed in this book are those of the author and do not necessarily represent or reflect the views of Celebrity Expert Author.

Contents

Journey. 12
Harden Not Your Hearts 15
Heart of the Matter 18
Don't Shoot the Messenger. 21
Help I've Fallen and I Can't Get Up 24
Great News 26
Rescue Me 28
Help I've Fallen Again 32
Separate Yourselves. 38
To Be Born Again or Not to Be Born Again 43
Don't Miss the Boat 47
Regrets? 53
Love, Love, Love 57
More Love 62
It's Already Here! 65
Awake! 71
Just Messengers? 74
Assuredly 76
Where Do We Go From Here? 80
Let's Try Here. 84
Divided You Fall. 89

7 Warnings..............................94
Contrary 98
These Works..........................102
Peace?.................................107
I Come Quickly.......................109
Prophecy 114
Warning Lights 117
How's Your Receiver?................121
It's So Easy...........................129
You Choose 133
It's Who You Know 138
There Is Hope........................140
Journey's End........................145

Prelude

You are probably asking yourself, why should I read this book, who is this person writing, and why should I believe what has been written?

Good questions and certainly ones that every Christian should be having when picking up any book.

1 Thes. 5:21
Test all things; hold fast what is good.

I am a servant of Jesus Christ, I have surrendered my life completely to Him, and I heard in my spirit that I can write and I can hear Him.

John 7:24
"Do not judge according to appearance, but judge with righteous judgement."

Several well-meaning Christians have been concerned as to where I have been receiving the information that I write. Please be assured that I have tested every thought in my spirit against the scriptures.

1 John 4:1
Beloved do not believe every spirit, but test the spirits, whether they are of God; because many false prophets have gone out into the world.

The first and foremost question as to why you should read this book lies beneath the lines of scripture.

Jer. 9:23,24
Thus says the Lord:

"Let not the wise man glory in his wisdom, Let not the mighty man glory in his might, Nor let the rich man glory in his riches;

But let him who glories glory in this, That he understands and knows Me, That I am the Lord, exercising loving kindness, judgement, and righteousness in the earth. For in these I delight," says the Lord.

You owe it to yourself to read this book of warnings from scripture and to draw your own conclusions with God.

I will take a brief a brief moment to explain the X in Journey. In the last few years there has been a TV show called X Factor which auditioned singing contestants to find that certain X factor in the contestants. Sport coaches are always on the look out for athletes with that certain extra quality. Successful business people are often said to display a certain unique X factor. Even the science world has coined the term X factor concerning a new catalyst for mineral absorption required for our health and well- being.

When Jesus began His ministry the world took notice and everyone from Kings to demons knew He was about. Jesus certainly demonstrated qualities that know one had ever seen before Him. Jesus also said that if you have seen Me you have seen the Father.

Prelude

Matt. 5:48
"Therefore you shall be perfect, just as your Father in heaven is perfect.

Those are pretty strong words of Jesus as He sums up the Sermon on the Mount. Jesus has asked us to walk and look as He did, with an undeniable, extra special X Factor difference.

Preface

I was in the Spirit during my morning prayer time and I heard these words; "You can write and you can hear Me". I have completed two books to date and this is the first titled Journey X.

Matt. 10:27
"Whatever I tell you in the dark, speak in the light; and what you hear in the ear, preach on the housetops.

This book reads very randomly as though my thoughts jump from one subject to another, because that is exactly how it happened.

Journey X contains our supernatural journey toward God. We have always had God to journey with, but the journey has rarely been ideal and rarely as desired by God, as free will has reigned. Perhaps the Lord chose me to write Journey X because of my mongrel blend of religion. I have a unique walk with Jesus that has taken me through several religious denominations and all the while I just wanted to love Jesus. I was not baptized until I was 29 years old.

I vaguely recall that I received Jesus when I was about 9 years old on our front lawn with my Baptist Missionary Aunt. I became a strange child who roamed the neighborhood looking for someone to take me to church on Sunday.

Preface

I eventually ended up at a United Church with a school class mate a couple of streets over.

My Grandpa Price intermittently took my cousin and I to a tiny Church of God where I vividly remember the songs and the warm sun beaming threw the church window I sat next to.

When I was a teenager my best friend's mother kidnapped us and took us to a large Pentecostal service where I ran to the front and gave myself to Jesus. I cried for hours but that became the extent of the experience.

Years later I encountered the Catholic Church which I was to embrace in order to get married. I studied, accepted and was baptized into the Catholic faith. I was very blessed to have a mother-in-law who introduced me to the charismatic movement of the Catholic church in the late 1980's and early 1990's. I grew and became so in love with Jesus. I was baptized in the Holy Spirit in 1991 and my life was never the same.

Life was good; I had immersed myself in a tiny local church where the Priest had become a good friend and confidant. I served the Lord through several Catholic organizations, taught Sunday school and even broke the Catholic rules to serve in another denominations Christian Women's group.

A few years later my life was uprooted to move to a province where I did not know the language and church services became meaningless. Shortly after the move, life took a severe detour and I was on my own raising 4 young children. Several of my Christian friends showed up for moral support but I was thrust to total dependence on Jesus. I recently heard a young Pastor say; "you don't know how much you need Jesus until He is all that you have". That is oh so true.

It would be tame to say that the whole experience was life altering but all these years later I can say that it was for the best and that without a doubt I could not have made the journey without Jesus. I was never closer to God, than when I was all alone.

I uprooted my life once more and moved to live close to family for my children. I resumed attendance with the Catholic Church, but the Charismatic movement had waned along with my spirit. I did become involved in church organizations but my heart longed for the Holy Ghost move.

A new neighbor invited us to an evening Pentecostal service and so once more the Holy Ghost got my attention. I used to say I was a Sunday morning Catholic and an evening closet Pentecostal. Needless to say; neither faith was happy with my disloyalty and I began a search for a new faith.

I had brief encounters with the Lutheran, Baptist and Anglican churches but none that could fill the great void I felt.

Many years later with my children now adults, I married my childhood sweetheart. Ironically, we had broken up as kids because he was Catholic and I was a heathen after all, according to his mother. We settled into a beautiful lakefront community which has one year-round Anglican church. I was still starving for some movement of the Holy Spirit somewhere.

One day (I'm quite sure by Divine appointment) we happened upon a main street non- denominational church in a nearby village. Halleluiah and Amen we found Jesus there.

We were blessed to find an on fire, Holy Ghost moving, real faith church. Thank you Jesus, for our Pastor Tim whom I think just might love You as much as I do.

This book includes my journey X and I pray you will experience a closer walk with Jesus through mine.

Journey

All the great sages and scholars through time have pondered the meaning of life.
Simply put life is a journey.

Prov. 5:21
For the ways of man are before the eyes of the Lord,
And He ponders all his paths.

The New World dictionary defines the word journey as:

1. The act or an instance of travelling from one place to another; trip

2. Any course or passage from one stage or experience to another

I personally think number two does a pretty good job at summing up my life.

As I am writing this my Dad is 91 years old and his memory is failing. He used to have a very funny saying that he would expound upon when he was having a deep moment. He would take a very deep breath; look me in the face and proclaim in his large deep voice "I want you to know that I predict …. Then his big voice would get even louder……. If things don't change they'll remain the same"

Pretty simple, right? Well; guess what I never really got the depth of the message.

It seems appropriate to mention at this point a popular definition of insanity.

"To do the same thing over and over expecting different results "

Discovering where we came from is essential to knowing where we are going.

Eph. 4:6
One God and Father of all, who is above all, and through all, and in you all

I am writing this as a born again Christian to my Christian brothers and sisters. Not from any religious point of view but from my own journey as a child of the One God.

I think that any Christian would have to confess that the ultimate destination of their journey is to arrive in heaven. To desire to go to heaven is as natural for us as the birds returning in spring. The birds after all were made by God and so were we. We come from God and the human search for the meaning of life comes full circle in our longing to return to God.

Prov. 19:21
There are many plans in a man's heart, Nevertheless the Lord's counsel —that will stand.

As I have written, Journey X is our journey toward God. Do you have what it takes to make the journey?

Prov. 16:25
There is a way that seems right to a man, But it's end is the way to death.

The scriptures speak no less than 10 times of "Harden Not Your Hearts".

Harden Not Your Hearts

Let's talk about the heart. We know obviously that the heart has to be in good working order or we are contemplating heaven. My King James Bible mentions the word heart in Proverbs 77 times and Ecclesiastes 40 times. I have not taken on the whole bible to date.

Prov. 16:9
A man's heart plans his way, But the Lord directs his steps.

Dr. Caroline Leaf noted Christian Doctor of neuroscience and author has uncovered some amazing God given qualities of the heart. Dr. Leaf's lifelong research indicates that your thoughts directly affect your heart. Neurologically, your heart reacts to what you think and feel. Your heart is not just a pump, but Dr. Leaf's research proves it to be like a second brain.

Science demonstrates that your heart has its own independent nervous system. It is extremely complex and referred to as the "brain of the heart".

There are at least 40,000 nerve cells in the heart – as many as are found in the various parts of the brain. Dr. Leaf states that her research is proving the heart to be a real intelligent force behind the thoughts and feelings we experience.

Further; the scientific evidence indicates that there are intricate lines of communication between the brain and the heart. The reality is that your heart is in constant communication with your brain and the rest of your body. The signals your heart sends to your brain influence not just perception and emotions but higher cognitive functions as well.

Prov. 3:3
Let not mercy and truth forsake you; Bind them around your neck, Write them on the tablet of your heart,

I recall a story some years ago about a little girl who was the recipient of a heart transplant. While recovering, she would awake screaming from a terrifying nightmare about being murdered. She would recant the exact horrific details of the murder including the face of her assailant each time she would waken from the nightmare. The Doctors dismissed the nightmares but the little girl's mother could not. I cannot recall who made the discovery but someone informed the mother that her daughter had received the heart of a young woman who had been brutally murdered and that the assailant had not been caught.

The ending to this story is that the little girl was able to identify the murderer to the police. He was caught and convicted and the little girl's nightmares subsided.

I think that this story will resonate with me forever.

I recently read the book called, "Heaven is for Real" which impacted me with another heart story. The book is about a four-year-old boy named Kevin who experiences heaven while undergoing life saving surgery. At one point in the story, Kevin sees a funeral casket and desperately questions his Dad, "Dad did he have Jesus in his heart, he had to have Jesus in his heart?"

Prov. 17:3
The refining pot is for silver and the furnace for gold, But the Lord tests the heart.

Heart of the Matter

I am overwhelmed by the incredible number of times that God uses the word heart throughout the scriptures.

It begins with the very first commandment to love the Lord your God with your whole heart, soul and strength.

Deut. 6: 5,6
You shall love the Lord your God with all your heart, with all your soul, and with all your strength

"And these words which I command you today shall be in your heart."

It is glaringly apparent throughout scripture that God deals with our hearts. It is also glaringly apparent that man throughout history has had a heart condition when it comes to God. The world is in desperate need of a heart transplant.

Deut. 5:29
Oh, that they had such a heart in them that they would fear Me and always keep all My commandments, that it might be well with them and with their children forever!

Rom. 10:10
For with the heart one believes unto righteousness,

and with the mouth confession is made unto salvation.

Now this heart condition of ours is not fatal, even when Peter told the Jews of how they had killed their Savior he gave them the way to be healed.

Acts 2: 37, 38
Now when they heard this they were cut to the heart, and said to Peter and the rest of the Apostles, Men and brethren, what shall we do?"

Then Peter said to them, "Repent and let every one of you be baptized in the name of Jesus Christ for the remission of sins; and you shall receive the gift of the Holy Spirit."

Scripture also tells us that if we would just ask that our loving God would give us our heart's desires. We are all very capable of asking, however; it is in the believing that we actually receive.

Matt. 17:20
So Jesus said to them, "Because of your unbelief, for assuredly, I say to you, if you have faith as a mustard seed, you will say to this mountain, move from here to there, and it will move; and nothing will be impossible for you.

And again, Jesus admonishes us about our heart condition.

Matt. 15:8
These people draw near to me with their mouth, And

honor Me with their lips, But their heart is far from Me.

There is not much I can add to this concerning the importance of our heart toward God save for these comforting words of Jesus.

Matt. 11:29
Take My yoke upon you and learn from Me, for I am gentle and lowly in heart, and you will find rest for your souls.

Wisdom is what God places in our hearts.

Prov. 2: 2,10
So that you incline your ear to Wisdom, And apply your heart to understanding;

When Wisdom enters your heart, And knowledge is pleasant to your soul,

Don't Shoot the Messenger

It's after midnight Wednesday which has been since the beginning of time a very, very early Thursday morning. Have you ever woken from sleep with something on your mind? This seems like a most impromptu time to speak about pigs or pork but let me tell you it feels even stranger to me. However, we need to talk about eating pork.

Statistics tell us that heart disease remains the number one killer in North America and cancer seems to be racing for the lead. Have you ever thought about why God commanded the Jewish people (His chosen for eternity) not to eat pig? God had Moses write down everything they should do and could eat to have the perfect healthy life God desired them to have. You know the whole cloven hoof, fish with scales menu. Well, pigs do have cloven hooves but they do not chew the cud.

Clean animals that chew their cud take up to 24 hours to refine their vegetation diet into flesh that we can and should eat. Pigs however which never limit their diet to vegetation will eat anything they can find including their own young and other dead pigs. Only 4 hours after the pig has dined on whatever; you will eat the same thing he did second hand. God made the pig to be scavengers not for human consumption.

Consider Dr. Rothschild's explanation of unclean foods. Do not consume any meat of scavenger animals comprising pork and all shellfish. First the meat of such animals is 10 times more perishable and difficult to preserve. Secondly the by-products that originate from digesting such scavenger meat are highly poisonous. He is referring to the so- called death enzymes such as cadaverine and putrescine. They are extremely useful to break down a corpse but not so in a living human body.

All edible meat can be and is hung for days to cure after it has been killed. Pork however starts its decomposition the very minute it dies. Do I need to say any more? I personally don't need convincing that God knew what He was talking about.

Isa. 65:3,4
A people who provoke Me to anger continually to My face; Who sacrifice in the gardens, and burn incense on the alters of brick;

Who sit among the graves, And spend the night in the tombs; Who eat swine's flesh, And the broth of abominable things in their vessels;

Now take a leap back to the Garden of Eden scene. God asked Adam and Eve to stay away from only one tree in the whole garden of trees for their own wellbeing. Do I hear a right? I know you have been telling yourself that you can't resist the smell of bacon and oh what about that Easter ham?

Ask yourself this. Does God only care about the Jewish people's health and wellbeing? Were Adam and Eve Jewish?

Deut. 14:6
You may eat every animal with cloven hooves, the hoof split in two parts, and that chews the cud, among the animals.

Remember how Dr. Caroline Leaf said we have two brains? One in our head and one in our heart. Jordan S. Rubin a doctor of naturopathic medicine has researched information that claims that our gut with over 100 million nerve cells may be responsible for how we feel. Maybe that old cliché saying about the way to a man's heart is threw his stomach is more true than we thought. Any way this information sure gives us a lot to chew on ha, ha.

God's word has been scientifically validated many times over. The laws of God are enforced and are as sure as the law of God's gravity. They were given by a loving God to save His people from physical devastation long before scientific principles of hygiene, viral transmission, bacterial infection or molecular cell physiology were understood.

Deut. 31:26, 27
"Take this Book of the Law, and put it beside the ark of the covenant of the Lord your God, that it may be there as a witness against you;

"for I know your rebellion and your stiff neck. If today, while I am yet alive with you, you have been rebellious against the Lord, then how much more after my death?

Help I've Fallen and I Can't Get Up

Before we become intimate with my journey, I would like to review some of man's journey with God. Aren't we always trying to justify our behavior?

Jesus did not die for us so that we could have Religion. He came to clean up the mess we created in the beginning in the Garden. He came to save us from ourselves.

It does not take a theologian to figure out what happened to mankind in the Garden. Satan had lost the battle in heaven to become greater than God and was thrown down to earth. God had given Adam and Eve the world so to speak. (Ha, Ha, Sorry) They were given authority over everything accept for this one and only one tree in the garden called the Tree of Knowledge of good and evil. You have to ask yourself why would they want the knowledge of evil? Now Satan who is eternally evil, knew how much God loved these two humans and that He had given them dominion over the earth and yes even over Satan. Eve had no knowledge of deception, of evil or the character of Satan. We need to cut Eve some slack, as she had absolutely never entertained one thought of disobedience or loftiness towards God. Satan contained the fullness of cunning and evil as he does today. Satan applied his greatest deception and in a moment of weakness and yes pride, Eve took her eyes off God. It was the first act of disobedience toward God and man has been trying to make up for it ever since. Yes: we still try to make up for it, even though the truth is that only Jesus could and did. Only Jesus mends this separation from God, and He did it once and for all.

Well you know the story; you know the ending. Strike one for man; homerun for Satan. Satan was handed over control of the earth, but that's not the end of the story.

Let's take a moment to think on the word obedience. If you are honest, you probably hate the word. I know I do. Unfortunately, through Eve's first disobedience we now retain the knowledge of good and evil. But do we really or have we spent history trying to forget?

Great News

Did we miss the broadcast? We are taught that Jesus died for our sins to make a way for us to heaven, but why do we ignore the fact that Jesus gave us His power and authority in this earth?

John 12:31
"Now is the judgement of this world; now the ruler of this world will be cast out.

Satan was defeated at the cross. You might be saying: yes I have heard that. Believe that Jesus said cast out of the world. Why are we still letting sin rule and ruin our lives?

John 8:34
Jesus answered them "Most assuredly, I say to you." Whoever commits sin is a slave of sin.

Jesus isn't just for Christmas. He isn't just the reason for the season. JESUS just the name of Jesus demons have to go.

The devil is working overtime to get us away from God and the not so good news is that he isn't having much of a problem.

Satan was defeated by our Savior Jesus and the word says we are once again above and not beneath Satan through our faith in Him. Jesus gave us back authority in the earth.

Satan got to Eve in the Garden but the big BUT is that Jesus made things right for us back to our God. We once again have access to all the Garden resources of God just for the asking under the cover of Jesus.

We struggle to control, solve and fix things all by ourselves when just like in the Garden all we need to do is ask. Just let go and let God. I know you're saying I struggle with trust issues but if you can't trust God why do you believe at all?

Rescue Me

Jesus said I came that you might have life and have it more abundantly.

Let's make it very clear here: Jesus did not bring any sickness or disease to punish nor did He take your loved one home to stop them from suffering.

> **John 10:10**
> *"The thief does not come except to steal and to kill and to destroy, I have come that they may have life, and that they may have it more abundantly.*

I want you to see that we have never been left alone or helpless after being banished from God's Garden.

> **Exo. 13:21**
> *And the Lord went before them by day in a pillar of cloud to lead the way, and by night in a pillar of fire to give them light, so as to go by day and night.*

The scriptures reveal glimpses of Jesus fighting on earth against Satan. Alongside of Jesus were His Angels especially Michael the Arch Angel.

> **Dan. 10:12, 13**
> *Then he said to me" Do not fear Daniel, for from*

the first day that you set your heart to understand, and to humble yourself before your God, your words were heard; and I have come because of your words

"But the Prince of the Kingdom of Persia withstood me twenty-one days; and behold Michael, one of the chief princes came to help me for I had been left alone there with the Kings of Persia.

The scriptures reveal a whole huge Thor like army out there at Jesus beckon call just for you and me.

Isa. 66:15
For behold, the Lord will come with fire And His chariots, like a whirlwind, To render His anger with fury, And His rebuke with flames of fire.

Dan. 10:20, 21
Then He said "Do you know why I have come to you? And now I must return to fight with the prince of Persia; and when I have gone forth, indeed the prince of Greece will come.

"But I will tell you what is noted in the scripture of truth. (No one upholds me against these, except Michael your prince.

Yes, we are in a daily battle for our very lives here on earth.

Eph. 6:12
For we do not wrestle against flesh and blood, but against principalities, against powers, against the rulers of

the darkness of this age, against spiritual hosts of wickedness in the heavenly places.

Did you get that? These hosts of wickedness are still battling in heavenly places! This war is not over. There will be yet a final battle for souls. It's time to make sure who's side you are helping.

Jesus's final words before His death were "it is finished'. Jesus defeated the devil on earth. Are you willing to pick up your sword and defend what Jesus gave His life for? We are talking about you. Your very soul.

John 17:15
I do not pray that you should take them out of the world but that you should keep them from the evil one.

There are 51 references to life in my concordance. Remember the Garden? In the midst of the garden, God planted the Tree of life.

The Tree of Life, in the center of the Garden is the reason Adam and Eve were turned out of the Garden. Angels were set at the entrance to guard anyone from entering again. The great news is that we have been given access to this Tree of knowledge through our faith in Christ Jesus.

Rev. 2:7
"He who has an ear, let him hear what the Spirit says to the churches. To him who overcomes I will give to eat from the Tree of life, which is in the midst of the Paradise of God."

Jesus came to lead us out of our Garden mentality and to show us how to make our journey home. Our final destination is not a place; it is God's eternal embrace.

Jesus's work is done on earth, and He is seated at His Father's right hand. He has not only given us His authority on earth as a reconciled child of God, but He has sent us the Holy Spirit as our teacher, guide and comforter. The Jewish nation were given God's laws in stone and a promised land. That hasn't worked out too well. It is not God's fault but that of a stiff- necked people and still God claims the Jewish people as His chosen ones. Do you have a stiff neck?

I don't believe it is coincidence that God gave His chosen people His laws on stone and that He warns us to harden not our hearts. We through the Holy Spirit can receive God's word into our hearts if we will but soften our hearts through our faith in Jesus. Our promised land will be in heaven.

Help I've Fallen Again

Throughout the scriptures God has spoken to mankind through the prophets and a very few chosen men of God who would talk and listen to Him directly.

As you can imagine after the great Garden scene mankind with no direction from God became pretty vile under the new rule of Satan.

Gen. 6:5
Then the Lord saw that the wickedness of man was great in the earth, and that every intent of the thoughts of his heart was only evil continually.

Gen. 6:7, 8
So the Lord said "I will destroy man whom I have created from the face of the earth, both man and beast, creeping thing and birds of the air, for I am sorry that I made them."

But Noah found grace in the eyes of the Lord.

I'm pretty certain you're familiar with this story as well?

Gen. 7:11
Then the Lord said to Noah "Come into the Ark, you and all your household, because I have seen that you are

righteous before Me in this generation. Now the flood waters came fifteen cubits upward and the mountains were covered.

Gen. 9:8, 9, 13

Then God spoke to Noah and to his sons with him saying:

"And as for Me, behold, I establish My covenant with you and your descendants after you.

"I set My rainbow in the cloud, and it shall be for the sign of the covenant between Me and the earth.

God promised that He would bear with all our wickedness and never flood the earth again. An interesting discovery for me was that God did not put the rainbow in the sky for me as a reminder of God's great mercy but as a reminder to Himself of His covenant even though we may have become as vile as the people in Noah's time.

About 600 years later, out of the genealogy of Shem from Noah came Abram; better known as Abraham (meaning father of many nations).

Now when Abram was 86 years old the Lord appeared to him in a vision. He told Abram "Look to heaven and count the stars if you are able to number them." And God said to him, "So shall your descendants be."

As you know there is another blaming wife story here. Abram's wife Sarai who was also in her 80's had given him no children and was doubtful concerning Abram's vision. Sarai became impatient waiting for Abrams promise from God, and convinced Abram to take her Egyptian handmaid in marriage. Egyptian blood for Jewish descendants? What was she thinking or perhaps not thinking?

Gen. 16: 5

Then Sarai; said to Abram, "My wrong be upon you! I gave my maid into your embrace; and when she saw that she had conceived, I became despised in her eyes. The Lord judge between you and me."

So now Sarai is blaming Abram for what has happened even though it was her idea to make things happen without God. Abram agrees to let Sarai handle the situation which we can assume was nasty as Hagar ran away.

Gen. 16: ,10,11,12

The Angel of the Lord said to her, "Return to your mistress, and submit yourself under her hand."

Then the Angel of the Lord said to her "I will multiply your descendants exceedingly, so that they shall not be counted for multitude."

And the Angel of the Lord said to her:

Behold, you are with child, And you shall bear a son. You shall call his name Ishmael, Because the Lord has heard your affliction.

He shall be a wild man; His hand shall be against every man, And every man's hand against him. And he shall dwell in the presence of all his brethren."

You have to wonder here if the above message from God's angel, might just have something to do with the conflict in the Middle East?

Once again the Lord appears to Abraham to assure him that he would have an heir at 99 years old and that Sarah would conceive this child. Sarah who was eavesdropping in on the conversation began to laugh. Hey, she was in her 90's.

Gen. 18:14

"Is anything too hard for the Lord? At the appointed time I will return to you, according to the time of life, and Sarah shall have a son."

As you know Sarah does conceive Isaac (whose name means laughter-appropriate right?) now becomes jealous of Hagar and Ishmael.

Gen. 21:10

Therefore she said to Abraham, "Cast out this bondwoman and her son; for the son of this bondwoman shall not be heir with my son, namely with Isaac."

Ladies I need you to see something here. We can lead our husbands down the garden path (Sorry I couldn't resist that one either) to walk in righteousness or unrighteousness. Men you can go to God as Abraham did and be assured your path will be steadfast.

Isaac would become the leader of his father's Jewish descendants and Ishmael the leader of his mother's people from Egypt to Saudi Arabia.

Gen. 15:18

On the same day the Lord made a covenant with Abram saying: "To your descendants I have given this land, from the River of Egypt to the great river, the river Euphrates.

Now is probably a good time to mention that the Muslim's profess that they are descendants of Abraham and they are correct. Their God is our God as is the God of the Jews, however; the defining difference is that the Jews did not recognize their Savior Jesus nor do the Muslims.

John 8:42

Jesus said to them, "If God were your Father, you would love Me, for I proceeded forth and came from God; nor have I come of Myself, but He sent Me.

About 700 years after Abraham; in the time of Rameses Moses led an estimated 600,000 Israelites out of Egypt. The Israelites witnessed 10 miraculous plagues by God, culminating in the death of all first- born Egyptians. In writing this last plague I can't help wondering if there is any connection between Ishmael the first born of Abraham and of the Egyptian nation? The Egyptian first born were in fact killed because they would not let God's chosen people return to their Promised Land. Just a thought.

God parted the Red Sea so that the Israelites could cross over to safety on dry land. God miraculously fed them every day with Manna from heaven. He made drinking water to come from rocks and He even provided quail in the desert when they complained about the Manna. There clothes never wore out and God Himself came amongst them to lead them by a cloud by day and a pillar of fire by night.

The Israelites had not a thing to worry about, right? God was leading them to the Promised Land and God Himself carved instructions in stone to take to their new lands. All they had to do was to listen to and obey God.

It took Moses 40 days up on Mount Sinai to receive written commandments from God. Down below the Israelites couldn't even make it 40 days before reverting back to worshipping Egyptian gods. It has been estimated that it took the Israelites 40 years to make an 11-day trip back to their promised land. Remember that promised land to Abraham?

Deut. 8:2
And you shall remember that the Lord your God led you all the way these 40 years in the wilderness to humble you and test you, to know what was in your heart, whether you would keep His Commandments or not.

Not even Moses made it to the Promised Land. It has been estimated that 600,000 Israelites left Egypt but only 40,000 went before the Ark of the Covenant into the Promised Land. Their whole journey had been miraculous, but they did not listen to God.

I would like to add a footnote here for the women in the crowd. We are taught that by one woman's disobedience sin came into the world, but never forget that by one woman's obedience our Lord and Savior was born.

Separate Yourselves

Some time ago I heard in my spirit to separate myself and I was questioning as to what impact that might have on my lifestyle. In this day and age, do we look different, or act differently as a believer in Jesus? I'm not talking about religious observances to fill a church pew. Is there a smile on your face and a song in your heart from your complete trust in and dependence on God? And yes, I am asking about during the difficult times and drama of life as well.

> **Rom. 12: 1,2**
> *I beseech you therefore, brethren by the mercies of God, which is your reasonable service,*
>
> *And do not be conformed to this world, but be transformed by the renewing of your mind, that you may prove what is that good and acceptable and perfect will of God.*

God has given us an average 75-80 years to make our journey to the Promised Land. Believe me when I say that I know how difficult the journey can become at times. But: have you ever been thrown into a lion's den full of ravenous man eating lions? Daniel from scripture was; but he trusted the God he knew to save him.

You probably have never been thrown into a furnace so hot that it killed anyone who got too close? Shadrach, Meshach and Abed-Nego were; but they trusted God to go against the Kings command unlike everyone else and walked out of that furnace unharmed and not even smelling of smoke.

Since mankind's journey began in the Garden, God has been trying to LOVE us into a perfect existence: to believe in, and trust in Him the One true and only God and Father of us all. If we had; there would have been no need for the prophets. If we had; God would not have had to sacrifice His Only Son.

Sadly; since time began (literally), we have struggled to be like God; refusing; instead of just receiving His love and blessings that He has tried to bestow upon us. God has had to talk to the Prophets to get messages to us, and ultimately He had to sacrifice His Only Son and save us from extinction.

2 Cor. 5:17
Therefore, if anyone is in Christ, he is a new creation; old things have passed away; behold, all things have become new

To believe God's word you must know it. The scriptures are the all-time, bestselling, most exciting, awesome, supernatural work you will ever read and yes dictated by God Himself.

The King James translation of the Bible was the most expensive and expansive book ever translated for us. King James had a vision to translate the Bible and he bankrupted his Kingdom to do it. He housed and paid the very best translators, scholars, linguists and Shakespearean writers from all of Europe. It took his lifetime and literally his life and fortune.

John 5:39
You search the scriptures for in them you think you have eternal life; and these are they which testify of me.

Would you say that Jesus was passive or aggressive? Hard question. Jesus's life was His witness. Know one has ever denied His love for His Father in heaven or His power. He is the scriptures fulfilled. Why do you believe that the greatest words ever written are kept out of the hands of our children, out of schools? Satan knows; it's the power and the witness that they contain. Even from a purely historical account He was the greatest man to walk the earth but He is not taught in our history books.

When my youngest children were attending a Catholic high school, there was an alarming incident that was handled even more alarmingly. Mutilating, dismembering, bodily threats were placed on-line concerning a few top students and athletes; my son was included. It turned out that a few disgruntled students who just happened to practice witchcraft at the school were the perpetrators. The police spoke to all the parents involved and fluffed the whole incident off as a teenage prank. Don't miss the point that they were allowed to practice witchcraft at school and to carry about their satanic books.

Now about that looking different! As I am writing this, maybe a hundred children are running by the front of our house with parents in tow. Our village is holding its annual free Easter egg hunt. What a celebration for children and what a worse demonstration by adults as to the meaning and celebration of Easter. Easter, it would seem has been reduced to Easter bunnies and chocolate. Do parents take the time any more to explain the enormity of Easter, our true gift of life? How God gave His One and only Son so that we all might live.

What about Christmas? It seems like Satan is not worried about this holiday either. Children are primed from babies to believe that it's all about Santa and gifts. We actually prepare them and convince them that Santa is the reason for the season. Guilty myself. All the while our greatest gift of the universe is reduced to a little manger, or Christmas carols sung once a year.

I know that Valentine's is really no big deal but it's because we have reduced it to chubby little cherubs shooting arrows and oh yes chocolate again. St. Valentine was a great saint who practised the art of loving and giving God's way.

Now I'm going to get into a highly celebrated day that North America goes crazy for and I hate; Halloween. First I want you to read the dictionary description of Halloween.

- all hallow even; hallow

- definite form of (halig) in sense holy person, hence saint

- The evening of Oct 31st which is followed by All Saints Day or Allhallows: now generally celebrated as fun making and masquerading

Now let's look at the definition of Hallowed:

- made holy or sacred; honored as holy; venerated

The first part of our Lord's Prayer starts with Hallowed Be Thy name. I think you can figure out where I was going with this one. What have we done? Danced around a golden calf?

It does seem that we have allowed our Christian celebrations to become pagan in nature, but a truly alarming fact is what we are allowing television to do to our children. I don't think I even need to go there if you have viewed some of the programming lately. Explicit sex, gay relationships, vampires, murders, and so on.

In a recent survey, children were asked about Daniel and the lion's den and the children thought it was the story from the lion king.

Rainbows and their true meaning have been reduced to a pot of gold, lucky charms cereal and dolls. Certainly, far from its true meaning of a judgement flood and the great mercy of God. Wait a minute maybe that's why we try to forget the true meaning of the rainbow; God's judgement.

As for what's on the internet I am not even going to go there because the thought of what our children find there sickens me.

Prov. 22: 6
Train up a child in the way he should go, And when he is old he will not depart from it.

To Be Born Again

Or

Not to Be Born Again

That is the big question.

John 3:3
Jesus answered and said to him, "Most assuredly, I say to you, unless one is born again, he cannot see the Kingdom of God."

Well that does seem pretty clear. The problem is that good intentioned Charismatic Christians have clichéd it to death. (Ha, Ha, sorry).

In the 1600's Brother Lawrence put it like this. "God is a Spirit; therefore; we must worship Him in spirit and in truth," He went on to say that we must present to God a true and humble spiritual worship in the very depth of our being.

Since the garden our flesh bodies carry the knowledge of sin, which is why Jesus says that we must die to our flesh. We must be born again of the Spirit, the very Spirit of God.

Only God's Spirit can keep us from sinning. God's Commandments were given to us so that we might know what is sin, but we do not have our own strength to keep from sinning. It is the very reason Jesus had to die on the cross for us.

John 3:6
"That which is born of the flesh is flesh, and that which is born of the Spirit is Spirit.

Acts 1:5
For John truly baptized with water, but you shall be baptized with the Holy Spirit not many days from now

Just before Jesus began his ministry on earth at the age of 33 He went to His cousin John the Baptist to be baptized. The water baptism which John was performing was for a sign of true repentance of sin. Jesus however; was not just baptized with water but the Holy Spirit came down from Heaven in the form of a dove.

Matt. 3:11
"I indeed baptize you with water unto repentance, but He who is coming after me is mightier than I, whose sandals I am not worthy to carry. He will baptize you with the Holy Spirit and fire.

It's not difficult. It merely means asking the Holy Spirit to come into your life and take up residence in your heart.
Repent of your sins and invite the Holy Spirit in. It should be "Christianity 101."
I am always amazed when people are reluctant to do this. To me it's like offering them a miracle cure to everything and

they say no thank you I'd rather stay sick. There is an apparent fear here and that comes from Satan himself. The devil knows the power and authority you will receive over him.

Acts 7:51
"You stiff-necked and uncircumcised in heart and ears! You always resist the Holy Spirit; as your fathers did, so do you.

Jesus needed the power of the Holy Spirit to overcome the attacks of Satan in the wilderness and to perform His miracle work on earth. We need the Holy Spirit for the exact same reason.

You do receive the Holy Spirit the very moment you confess Jesus as your Savior, however; the power to keep journeying toward God, the power to witness, the very power and authority of Jesus comes only through the Baptism of the Holy Spirit.

Does anyone know where the baptizing of babies came from? God knows the heart of every single human being ever born and to be born on this earth. Does anyone actually believe that our most merciful God would allow an unbaptized child to go to hell?

Indeed; to be baptized in the Holy Spirit requires a willing heart, a true willingness to surrender your will to God's. I am not sure why some believer 's need time in their journey with God to make this surrender? It is a great leap of faith. Do we harbor pride, or fear? If it is fear that you feel, know that this fear is of the devil. The same fear that came upon Adam in the Garden. Don't let the devil keep you from your greatest journey.

Gen. 3:10
So he said, " I head Your voice in the garden, and I was afraid because I was naked; and I hid myself."

There are two kinds of faith, one in our head or intellectual faith and the one necessary for our salvation, in your heart. Your heart responds to all things of relationship and we must have a personal relationship with Jesus for true saving faith.

James 2:18,19
But some will say, "You have faith, and I have works." Show me your faith without your works, and I will show you my faith by my works.

You believe that there is one God. You do well. Even the demons believe- and tremble!

You need great faith to respond to Jesus and with that comes great victory and great works for the Lord. I believe that it is true to claim, that all who have received the gift of the Holy Spirit can mark the day and hour.

Don't Miss the Boat

It's very interesting to me to ask someone if they think they are going to heaven. Some respond with a shoulder shrug while some say I certainly hope so. Very few give a resounding yes and amen sister.

Thank you God, that your Son Jesus settled this issue once and for all by the sacrifice of Himself.

In the time of Noah, it is recorded that the people were vile and evil much as it is now. It took Noah and his sons over 100 years to complete the Ark and all the while Noah a preacher of righteousness was inviting others to be saved.

2 Peter 2:5
And did not spare the ancient world, but saved Noah, one of eight people, a preacher of righteousness, bringing in the flood on the world of the ungodly;

Once Noah, his family and all God's creatures were inside the Ark; Scripture says that the Lord shut the door of the Ark. The doors that God shuts no man can open.

God doesn't send us to hell, He simply shuts the door to heaven. Maybe you're telling yourself wright now "I'm a good person", I'll go to heaven when I die.

Jesus spoke often about doors to heaven and about keys to heaven.

Matt. 16:19

"And I will give you the of the keys of the Kingdom of heaven, and whatever you bind on earth will be bound in heaven, and whatever you loose on earth will be loosed in heaven.

God Himself through the Holy Spirit wants to tell you to get into the boat. Noah built the Ark. The Israelites had the Ark to carry the covenant of God and you are the Ark that carries the Holy Spirit.

We are told that when we accept Jesus Christ into our heart, and believe He is the Son of God, we can be certain that we will go to heaven when we die.

Don't just have Jesus in your head. You must have Jesus in your heart. As scripture says, a new heart not a hardened heart.

Now my spirit is being prompted to add these words of Jesus.

I have written the whole scripture below that outlines how we must use what the Lord has given us or as the ending warns, we will be thrown out into the darkness.

Matt. 25: 13-30

"Watch therefore, for you know neither the day nor the hour in which the Son of man is coming.

"For the kingdom of heaven is like a man travelling to a far country, who called his own servants and delivered his goods to them.

"And to one he gave five talents, to another two, and

to another one, to each according to his own ability; and immediately he went on a journey.

"Then he who had received the five talents went and traded with them, and made another five talents.

"And likewise he who had received two gained two more also.

"But he who had received one went and dug in the ground, and hid his lord's money.

"After a long time the Lord of those servants came and settled accounts with them.

"So he who had received the five talents came and brought five other talents, saying Lord you delivered to me five talents; look I have gained five more talents besides them.

"His lord said to him, well done good and faithful servant; you were faithful over a few things, I will make you ruler over many things. Enter into the joy of your lord.

"He also who had received two talents came and said, Lord you delivered to me two talents; look I have gained two more talents besides them.

"His lord said to him, Well done good and faithful servant; you have been faithful over a few things, I will make you ruler over many things. Enter into the joy of your lord.

> "Then he who had received the one talent came and said, Lord, I knew you to be a hard man, reaping where you have not sown, and gathering where you have not scattered seed.
>
> And I was afraid and went and hid your talent in the ground. Look, there you have what is yours.
>
> "But his lord answered and said to him, You wicked and lazy servant, you knew that I reap where I have not sown, and gathered where I have not scattered seed.
>
> So you ought to have deposited my money with the bankers, and at my coming I would have received back my own with interest.
>
> Therefore take the talent from him, and give it to him who has ten talents.
>
> For to everyone who has, more will be given, and he will have abundance; but from him who does not have, even what he has will be taken away.
>
> And cast the unprofitable servant into the outer darkness. There will be weeping and gnashing of teeth.

We have all been given talents by God, some menial, some miraculous but some.

You may not have figured them out exactly, but the above scripture does not dwell on the talents but knowing the Master. If you truly know your Master, you will give Him what is expected, and in doing so, you will be given more.

Perhaps this scripture has a much more powerful conviction against presumption! Have we been ignoring our God given talents? Do we presume that we are doing enough with our religious rituals? If we presume that we know God, are we doing what He has asked of us? Pretty convicting questions, but if heaven is at stake, ones we should be asking ourselves, in light of the above scripture.

Matt. 23:13
"But Woe to you, scribes and Pharisees, hypocrites! For you shut up the kingdom of heaven against men; for you neither go in yourselves, nor do you allow those who are entering to go in.

Matt. 24:5
"For many will come in My name, saying "I am the Christ", and will deceive many.

Are you up for the mission? If you accept this mission these words will self-destruct in 5 seconds. (Sorry I watch too many movies).

James 1:22
But be doers of the word, and not hearers only, deceiving yourselves.

In the last 50 years, we seemed to have dropped the fire and brimstone teachings, especially concerning hell. Jesus does however, teach us many times the ways of heaven and the requirements to get in.

Matt. 19:24

"And again I say to you it is easier for a camel to go through the eye of a needle than a rich man to enter the kingdom of God."

Matt. 20:16

"So the last will be first, and the first last. For many are called but few chosen.

Matt. 25: 33,34,41

"And He will set the sheep on His right hand, but the goats on the left.

"Then the King will say to those on His right hand, "Come you blessed of My Father, inherit the kingdom prepared for you from the foundation of the world:

"Then He will also say to those on the left hand, "Depart from Me, you cursed, into the everlasting fire prepared for the devil and his angels:

We are all part of God's great plan either enjoying salvation or facing judgement but the decision is always ours.

On our journey, neglected opportunities bring regrets. Missing heaven would be our final and never ending regret.

Regrets?

Scripture in Revelation 21:27 says that one day the doors of Heaven will be shut against the evil world.

Jesus often spoke in Parables, as in the one of the ten virgins. In it the Kingdom of God is likened to a marriage.

Matt. 25:6
"And at midnight a cry was heard; Behold the bridegroom is coming; go out to meet him!

Each one of the ten virgins had the same opportunity to keep their lamp full of oil and to wait in anticipation for the bridegroom. The parable goes on to say that five virgins were ready with extra lamp oil and five were not when the cry came at midnight. (a most unlikely time)

So obviously five virgins were ready and went in with the bridegroom to the marriage and the door was shut while the other five were outside looking for more oil to buy.

Matt. 25:13
Watch therefore, for ye know neither the day nor the hour wherein the Son of Man cometh.

In the early church, God was pouring out His Spirit and in the midst was a couple named Ananias and Saphira.

Acts 5:3,5

But Peter said "Ananias, why has Satan filled your heart to lie to the Holy Spirit and keep back part of the price of the land for yourself?

Then Ananias hearing these words, fell down and breathed his last. So great fear came upon all those who heard these things.

Ananias's wife repeated the lie to Peter and also died. They both missed their opportunity because of sin or wrong doing.

Sin or just being too busy with living (not life) will always cause regrets. We must have our heart and mind listening for God so that we can know what good plan He has for us. We must know what the scriptures say about God and to us as warnings and sign posts. We must always be ready for the day when He comes to take us home or when He returns.

James 1:19-21

So then my beloved brethren, let every man be swift to hear, slow to speak, slow to wrath;

For the wrath of man does not produce the righteousness of God

Therefore lay aside all filthiness and overflow of wickedness, and receive with meekness the implanted word, which is able to save your souls.

All our prayers cannot save souls. Clearly scripture says that we must choose whom we will serve.

Josh. 24:15

And if it seems evil to you to serve the Lord, choose for yourselves this day whom you will serve, whether the gods which your fathers served that were on the other side of the River, or the gods of the Amorites, in whose land you dwell. But as for me and my house we will serve the Lord.

The door of opportunity is open to each person to choose his destiny. Jesus has said that He stands at the door!

It is as certain as taxes they say, that we will all leave this earth one day. We are the ones that choose where we will arrive. There is heaven to gain and hell to shun.

Perhaps you plan to live the good earthly life and make the big end game play? Why do we make serving God become such a burden for us?

I think it's important to say here that we need to start enjoying the journey and not live waiting for the destination.

Deut. 30:19, 20

"I call heaven and earth as witnesses today against you, that I have set before you life and death, blessing and cursing; therefore choose life, that both you and your descendants may live.

"that you may love the Lord your God, that you may obey His voice, and that you may cling to Him, for He is your life and the length of your days; and that you may dwell in the land which the Lord swore to your fathers, to Abraham, Isaac, and Jacob, to give them"

If you know Jesus, you must know how much He wants to greet you in Heaven? It's your journey. What plans have you made so far?

Don't forget that He saved us not on the basis of our deeds but according to His mercy. You don't need to be working towards Heaven but receiving towards Heaven. Just receive your reservation and enjoy the ride on the way.

Titus 3: 5, 6

Not by works of righteousness which we have done, but according to His Mercy He saved us, through the washing of regeneration and renewing of the Holy Spirit,

Whom He poured out on us abundantly through Jesus Christ our Savior

Love, Love, Love

As the old song goes all you really need is love. It is strange to me that we seem to get so many things in life backwards. Jesus's way is also backwards to today's way of living. Is this perhaps why we find it so difficult to accept it?

The Jewish people found it unbelievable to accept Jesus as their Savior because they were expecting a King. Jesus was in fact betrayed by one of His own for silver. Are we betraying our Lord for the things of this world? Let's take each one of Jesus's Sermon on the Mount and compare it to life today.

Matt. 5: 3, 4, 5, 6, 7, 8, 9, 10
Blessed are the poor in spirit, for theirs is the kingdom of heaven

None of us can truly know, but it would appear that we are in the greatest "Me" crisis of the world. Poor Me! Well it doesn't sound like poor me. The day of the self-made man. Look out for number one. If it feels good do it. Swallow your pride: I think not. I'm not certain but I don't believe any of these statements qualify for the poor in spirit.

Blessed are those who mourn for they shall be comforted

Today we like to comfort ourselves. We self- medicate, pop a pill; have a drink; go shopping; have some chocolate or perhaps a pity party with some friends and chocolate.

Blessed are the meek for they shall inherit the earth

Have you ever heard these words? Stand up for your rights: go over his head to his boss: make your mark in life; do whatever it takes; take him for all he's worth; don't let them walk all over you. Just asking?

Blessed are those who hunger and thirst for righteousness, for they shall be filled

Ever had one of these thoughts? I don't want to rock the boat; I need this job; you can't fight the government; I don't want to get involved; it's none of my business; I just don't have the time.

Blessed are the merciful for they shall obtain mercy

Well I bet this one came to mind quickly?" Show No Mercy"; they deserved everything they got; he had it coming; who do they think they are?

Blessed are the pure in heart, for they shall see God

Now this is actually the most difficult one. What is a pure heart? We were created in Gods image. Image is like the reflection in a mirror. We are like a slanted mirror, created to receive Gods glory, love and likeness and reflect it back into the world.

> *Blessed are the peacemakers, for they shall be called the sons of God*

I don't believe that we are the worst generation for war and killing but perhaps the worst for judging our brothers and sisters. We make comparisons of everything from lifestyle, looks, income, bank accounts, houses, spouses, work and just about anything you can name. You name it we have a comment for it.

> *Blessed are those who are persecuted for righteousness sake for theirs is the kingdom of heaven*

Are you having trouble finding Christmas cards that mention Christ? Are you excluded from work parties because you're one of them? Christians. With television and internet, we are constantly being made aware of this one today, one I could never imagine would happen here. Many factions are presently persecuting and killing all over the world those who stand firm in their Christian beliefs. The recent attacks of ISIS have come very close to home.

Scripture says all the ways of a man are right in his own eyes. You cannot judge yourself by your own standards or your own righteousness, but only through His eyes.

2 Chron. 16:9
For the eyes of the Lord run to and fro throughout the whole earth, to show Himself strong in the behalf of them whose heart is perfect toward Him. Herein thou hast done foolishly: therefore from henceforth thou shalt have wars.

Now again about having things backwards. You know how we say that a dog is man's best friend; spell dog backwards and you have your true best friend.

2 Tim. 3: 1-4

But know this, that in the las days perilous times will come:

For men will be lovers of themselves, lovers of money, boasters, proud, blasphemers, disobedient to parents, unthankful, unholy,

unloving, unforgiving, slanderers without self- control, brutal despisers of good,

traitors, headstrong, haughty, lovers of pleasure rather than lovers of God;

Do you think maybe we have arrived to these perilous times? Well don't stress, love is the answer.

1 John 4:8

He who does not love does not know God, for God is love.

We talk about love in the church, but there is oh so little of it. We talk about the pastor, each other, and rarely visit or pray for our Christian brothers and sisters. Do we help at soup kitchens or visit the sick in hospital? Our flesh is inherently selfish and self-centered. We need to start a war with ourselves, or better still, be so in love with Jesus that we see Him in everyone. It does sound backwards but the way to get over yourself is to reach out to others in need.

If you want to be happy, live to make someone else happy. Backwards thinking.

1 Cor. 13:2

And though I have the gift of prophecy, and understand all mysteries and all knowledge, and though I have all faith, so that I could remove mountains, but have not love I am nothing.

Matt. 5: 44 & 46

But I say to you, love your enemies, bless those who curse you, do good to those who hate you, and pray for those who spitefully use you and persecute you.

For if you love those who love you, what reward have you? Do not even the tax collectors do so?

More Love

We are all born with a hole in our heart that only God can fill. He plugs it with Himself – perfect Love

1 John 4: 18,19
There is no fear in love; but perfect love casts out fear, because fear involves torment

But he who fears has not been made perfect in love.

There is an old saying that love makes the world go around. Well I think perhaps todays definitions of love just may be what is wrong with the world.

Let me give you just a few of my dictionary definitions:

- to be fond of, desire

- a deep and tender feeling of affection, or attachment, or devotion to

- a strong liking for or interest in

- a strong usually passionate, affection of one person for another based in part on sexual attraction

Personally, I have never read such weak, passionless words to describe love. Perhaps that is exactly why people are having difficulty with relationships and marriage. They don't have a real description of love and they have never experienced it either.

Scripture says that the Holy Spirit came to fill our hearts with God's true Love. A love story, an eternal marriage for which we are all born that no one would enter eternity alone.

I guess we have always claimed that it is difficult to describe true love. Well I know one thing for sure it is not lukewarm or weak.

This morning I woke up praying and asking God for His definition of love.

Here goes:

Caring so deeply for every single aspect of another that you completely forego the aspects of oneself even unto death.

Now just imagine a marriage where both are fulfilling God's definition of Love!

I don't wish to take the romance out of love, but love really is a choice. It doesn't just happen, or fall on you. It is the single largest personal commitment an individual will ever make.

Just as our young people seem to be having great difficulty in making commitments today, and yes to getting married I do understand their fear. They have a fear, perhaps because they understand in part this huge commitment to give up part of oneself and perhaps that's why they have not experienced true love.

Self, Self, Self

Dictionary description of Selfish:

- too much concerned with one's own welfare or interests and having little or no concern for other's

Now I hear a lot of s's hear and when I hear the ssss sound I think of sssssnakes and Satan the worst snake of them all. Oh how he wooed mankind with himself from the beginning in the garden.

Now I want to talk about a dirty word in society today; obedience.

Dictionary description of obedient:

- suggests a giving in to the orders or instructions of one in authority or control

- suggests a weakness of character that allows one to yield meekly to another's request or demand.

Does it sound like the snake had a hand in writing that one?

Why do we find it so difficult to be obedient? That old ssself. Self wants to do what feels good for self. "Just Do It"

Obedience is not an event but a way of life. Many of the past Saints practiced selfless love. I'm sure many names will come to mind. It is most curious to me how many of them were named Theresa. You may be saying to yourself only saints had enough self-control to be saints. Don't forget we are all called saints in Christ Jesus. The Holy Spirit has given us control over our flesh, true freedom and yes self-control to choose.

If God is love and love is a gift, the giver and the gift are one.

It's all about the love. There is only love in heaven. You can't be born into it, but only born again into it; but it can't happen without you choosing and receiving the gift.

It's Already Here!

Although the Holy Spirit has probably been dropping alert bombs on me, it took a gifted young man of God to finally penetrate my intellect and heart. Jefferson Bethke is a very young author full of the ancient wisdom of God. Not what you would expect from such a young man but isn't that just how God works?

If you are as old as I am you will remember the 1960's and the Vietnam War. Young US men were being drafted into a war that they knew little about and in most cases, did not want to participate in. Young people all over North America made the peace sign with their fingers and chanted "make love not war". Well most adults just dismissed us as pot smoking hippies.

In Jefferson's book (It's not what you think) my spirit was finally invaded not just to the fact that our whole way of life is contrary to God's kingdom, but that we've even got the journey wrong. I have been contemplating life's difficult journey toward heaven for some time. I'm always trying to make sure I don't mess up the trip.

Well here is my aha moment. God hasn't been trying to get us to heaven; He has been trying to get heaven to us.

What does the Lord's Prayer given to us by Jesus say?

Our Father who art in heaven

Hallowed be thy name

"Thy Kingdom come"

Thy will be done on earth as it is in heaven

Hmm!

We are always reaching up to heaven for help when God has already sent heaven down to us. It is only when we completely receive His true love – Jesus – we find heaven on earth.

2 Peter 3: 13, 14
Nevertheless we, according to His promise, look for new heavens and a new earth in which righteousness dwells.

Therefore, beloved, looking forward to these things, be diligent to be found by Him in peace, without spot and blameless;

If indeed the Christian world lived according to God's word, according to the Commandments, the Sermon on the Mount, would we not experience heaven on earth? Would not every non- believer envy our life and want what we have? The Israelites were envied and persecuted because of their Divine providence and protection and health.

I'm switching gears here and going to talk about a subject that may be keeping some of us from God's perfect will.

Most of us are intrigued by the Supernatural. Some go to the extreme and delve into Wiji Boards, tarot cards and fortune tellers, but we know only in part there is something to it. A warning here first!

> **Deut. 18: 10, 11, 12**
> *There shall not be found among you anyone who makes his son or daughter pass through fire, or one who practices witchcraft, or a soothsayer or one who interprets omens or a sorcerer,*
>
> *Or one who conjures spells, or a medium, or a spiritist, or one who calls up the dead.*
>
> *For all who do these things are an abomination to the Lord, and because of these abominations the Lord your God drives them out from before you.*

Okay then! We know in part and understand in part how God operates in two realms or two Kingdoms. The earth and flesh and blood and Heaven and the Spiritual realm. Be warned that we can be affected by the evil spiritual realm and not even be aware of it. If a believer crosses that line into the dark spiritual realm here on earth, they are letting in something that they alone cannot handle. We need the continual revelation and protection of the Holy Spirit within us. We are not alone on this earth. We have the constant evil eye of Satan watching our every move, and ready to pounce, should we stumble. Always remember the scripture that says "Just the name of Jesus, demons have to flee"

Just as Satan tempted Jesus as He fasted in the desert, he will most often show up just as you are about to make a spiritual decision. Brother Andre of Montreal was a very small in stature Catholic Brother who was daily bothered by Satan. It was reported by staff in the house that on occasion he would be physically dragged out of bed and sometimes pushed up a wall by an invisible force. Brother Andre was reported to laugh and say that he must be going to do something great for God today.

To receive supernatural healing, wisdom, understanding, and divine protection, we have to be in God's supernatural sphere. This is not something to be feared or dismissed nor placed at the level of fortune-tellers. It is how our Almighty God operates.

> ***2 Kings 6:17***
> *And Elisha prayed, and said, "Lord, I pray, open his eyes that he may see." Then the Lord opened the eyes of the young man, and he saw. And behold, the mountain was full of horses and chariots of fire all around Elisha.*

I'm certainly not writing any of this to turn anyone off, or dismiss it as radical but only to further point out that God has not only been trying to put heaven's resources into our hands but has come down Himself to guide and protect.

When Daniel was praying for his people and Israel and pleading to God, Jesus Himself came to Daniel.

> ***Dan. 10:12***
> *Then He said to me, do not fear Daniel, for from the first day you set your heart to understand, and to humble yourself before God, your words were heard; and I have come because of your words.*

Now check out verse 13 to understand just how much goes on around us in the spiritual realm.

Dan. 10:13

But the prince of the kingdom of Persia withstood me twenty-one days; and behold, Michael, one of the chief princes, came to help me, for I had been left alone there with the Kings of Persia.

In conclusion, we need to realise the powerful workings of God going on in the Spirit realm that co-exists here on earth with us. There is a bigger and better Thor like army of God, fighting and protecting His Chosen on earth.

There are similarities of all the end time prophets, but none more striking of that between Daniels and the end time prophecies of John. They are given as warnings to mankind to return to God. Timelines and events are from God and from His spiritual realm, not our earthly calendar.

The supernatural battle has raged through our history books, but we have written them purely from our human perspective. Take off the blinders and see God through history and you will be awed by His power and protection.

Rev. 9:11

And they had over them the angel of the bottomless pit, whose name in Hebrew is Abaddon, but in Greek he has the name Apollyon.

Rev. 17:17

"For God has put it into their hearts to fulfill His purposes, to be of one mind, and to give their kingdom to the beast, until the words of God are fulfilled.

Heavenly forces are here on earth, just as sure as God is in you when you surrender to Him.

Isn't it just the very opposite once more. Your surrender opens the door to your complete protection. We are never told to kill ourselves with over thinking and doing but in fact die to ourselves in complete surrender to God's perfect way.

Awake!

I ended the last chapter with the message of surrender for protection. Kind of a God oxymoron. I know this whole idea of surrendering yourself seems a bit frightening. Let go of yourself to be your true self. Let's look at the definition of surrender.

- to give up possession of or power over; yield to another on demand or compulsion

- to give up claim to; give over or yield esp. voluntarily, as in favor of another

- to give up or abandon

- to yield or resign (oneself) to an emotion, influence

In the above description is the repetitive word give. It is only in the act of giving ourselves to God that He gives us Himself.

For some time now my spirit has been hounded by the word Awake.

1 Cor. 15:34
Awake to righteousness, and do not sin: for some do not have the knowledge of God. I speak this to your shame.

Awake

- a merging of two words
- to rouse from sleep
- to rouse from inactivity; activate; stir up
- to call forth
- to make aware

The pressing reminder of the word awake has given me an urgency to get this book completed.

Prov. 3:12
For whom the Lord loves, He corrects, even as a father corrects the son in whom he delights

Just as the world seems to be at the pinnacle of self-love on the flip side of society are those who struggle with self-hatred. Both of these thought processes are equally damaging to one's soul. Pain is inevitable in life, but misery is always an option.

Jesus told us that we must repent. We are not asked to feel one way or the other, but to simply stop doing what is contrary to God's word. Repentance is a re-alignment to the will and word of God.

We will never think too highly of ourselves if we remember the One who is the giver of our blessing, and we will not remain in our shame if we remember the One who has died for us.

Heb. 9:27

And it is appointed for men to die once, but after this the judgement

As long as there is evil there has to be judgement
Is it time for true repentance?

Rev. 22:12

And behold I am coming quickly, and My reward is with Me, to give to everyone according to his work

How far away are you from eternity?
One heartbeat!

Just Messengers?

Angels were created like ourselves for God's intended purposes. We've read that some are to praise and worship Him, some as God's messengers and some appear to be for our protection. How can we not believe in angels when the scriptures mention them almost 4 dozen times?

> **Heb. 1: 4, 7**
> *Having become so much better than the angels, as He has by inheritance obtained a more excellent name than they*
>
> *And of the angels He says: "Who makes His angel's spirits and His ministers a flame of fire."*

God's greatest angel Lucifer through his pride was cast down to earth with one third of God's angels. Satan refers to God's angels himself.

> **Matt. 4:6**
> *And said to Him, "If you are the Son of God throw Yourself down. For it is written: "He shall give His angels charge over you.*

Angels are here on earth and have been sent by God to protect us. Jesus Himself could call down legions.

Just Messengers?

Matt. 26:53

Or do you think that I cannot now pray to My Father, and He will provide Me with more than 12 legions of angels?

My mother recently passed and I spent several hours at her bedside in the hospital. A day or so before her passing I was praying at her bedside, when as real as if in the flesh I sensed and saw 3 male figures at the end of her bed hugging and greeting each other. I was curious, so I asked; are you the angel of death?

I surprised them by my awareness of their presence but one answered and said: no, there is no such angel. He informed me that there were angels there to take my mother home. The third angel returned to the person in the bed next to my mother's and at that moment a nurse came in and everyone disappeared from my sight. I do need to mention here that my mother's anxious condition subsided at the arrival of the angels. It is well known and documented by nurses that their patients condition of anxiety lessons just before death. It should not be surprising that God would not let any soul die alone.

Matt. 16: 22

"So it was that the beggar died, and was carried by the angels to Abraham's bosom. The rich man also died and was buried.

Matt. 18:10

Take heed that you do not despise one of these little ones, for I say to you that in heaven their angels always see the face of My Father who is in heaven.

Assuredly

Matt. 6: 5,6

"And when you pray, you shall not be like the hypocrites. For they love to pray standing in the synagogues and on the corners of the streets, that they may be seen by men. Assuredly, I say to you, they have their reward."

But when you pray, go into your room, and when you have shut your door, pray to your Father who sees you in secret and will reward you openly.

The Jewish people certainly get one thing very right. They study and know their Torah (their laws) and teach them to their children. I am so sad to be at this age of my life and to finally be truly studying the scriptures. The best part is that my Lord Himself is teaching me.

Matt. 6: 7, 9

"And when you pray do not use vain repetitions as the heathen do. For they think they will be heard for their many words.

"In this manner therefore pray: Our Father in heaven, Hallowed be Your name.

This prayer went on to be the cornerstone prayer of the Christian church. The Lord's Prayer.

I'm not sure why some churches have chosen to drop this prayer from their services? I certainly pray that it is not because they think they have outgrown it. On the other hand, the heartless repetition of this prayer in some church services is not any better. If you were to take the time and study each line of this prayer you would not only be grateful for it but realize it's completeness for our life.

St. Theresa of Avila said that in His prayer the Lord begins to give us His Kingdom on earth, so that we may truly praise Him and Hallow His name. St Theresa also warns to truly reverence this prayer as we are calling God's Kingdom down into our hands.

1 John 3:1
Behold what manner of love the Father has bestowed upon us, that we should be called children of God! Therefore the world does not know us, because it did not know Him.

Our Father in heaven,

Hallowed be Your name.

You can be sure you are truly praising Him and Hallowing His name since you are glorifying the Lord as a member of His household. His child.

Your kingdom come.

Your will be done on earth as it is in heaven.

The great chasm between heaven and earth has been bridged. Jesus stands in the gap.

John 17: 17
That they all may be one, as You Father, are in Me, and I in You; that they also may be one in Us, that the world may believe that You sent Me.

Give us day by day our daily bread.

This is not real bread, or even the manna from heaven sent to sustain the Israelite's on their journey through the desert; but the true bread of life.

John 6: 33,35
For the bread of God is He who comes down from heaven and gives life to the world.

And Jesus said to them, I am the bread of life. He who comes to Me shall never hunger; and he who believes in Me shall never thirst.

St. Theresa said it beautifully: God has given us this most holy Bread, forever as the sustenance and manna of humanity.

And forgive us our sins,

For we also forgive everyone who is indebted to us.

Our Lord knows that this virtue to forgive, this mutual love, is the hardest to attain but the dearest to His heart.

And do not let us into temptation,

But deliver us from the evil one.

I hope you noticed that I changed lead us not to let us not? Several years ago a Christian writer pointed out that God is not capable of leading us into temptation and I had to agree with him. Satan is out there folks, just looking for the moment to ruin our journey.

James 1:13
Let no one say when he is tempted, "I am tempted by God"; for God cannot be tempted by evil, nor does He Himself tempt anyone.

How very opposite we live to the will of God. Again St. Theresa points out: His will is for us to desire truth, whereas we desire falsehood; His will is for us to desire the eternal whereas we desire that which passes away; His will is for us to desire great and sublime things whereas we desire the base things of the earth; He would have us desire only what is certain whereas here on earth we desire what is doubtful. What a mockery it all is unless we beseech God to deliver us from all evil.

Gods will must be done in heaven and on earth. There are so many hindrances on earth to the enjoyment of so many blessings from heaven. Don't be afraid to pray that God's will be done; He gives us the Kingdom while we are still alive.

Lastly St. Theresa said: no one who has experienced the Kingdom of God on earth will be content to do his own will but to do the will of the King.

Where Do We Go From Here?

Yesterday I became a little overwhelmed with all the notes I had made for this book. I was about to begin a new as yet unwritten chapter about the Ten Commandments. Now I know you're probably thinking Oh No not a lecture on the commandments.

Well I actually have been stressing over how to disguise this chapter. Should I call it the Big 10? The Law? and so on; when these words in the title invaded my thoughts.

Where do we go from here?

Don't panic I'm not going to list the commandments here although you may want to give them a read at the end of this chapter.

1 John 5:3
For this is the love of God, that we keep His commandments. And His commandments are not burdensome.

In these latter days referred to in scriptures, we are a generation of great wealth, education and scientific advances. On the flip side of this generation we have so much disease, illness, corruption and evil intent.

We boast of the most Christian denominations and demonstrate the least faith in God.

Starting in the late 1960's the United States has ridden a huge wave to remove God, firstly from their schools, then courtrooms and just about every public place you can imagine. Canada has been getting on this wave as well.

The Ten Commandments (God's Laws) given to us by God; erased from before God's people who so desperately need them. Who ordered this? The very people who obviously need them the most? So, as the story of the Wild West goes; remove the laws and the lawlessness rises. Bring on the guns!

Rom. 3:20
Therefore by the deeds of the law no flesh will be justified in His sight, for by the law is the knowledge of sin.

I know that everyone who is reading this book is aware of the alarming increase in violence not only in the streets but in our schools. So let me ask you this; if all the references to God and His Laws are removed from the public areas and especially schools, just where will future generations learn any morality and of God?

Church attendance is declining and the great tent Evangelists are dead or dying off. Our children are being threatened not to display their Christian faith and yes shockingly even shot at on account of it.

In court rooms where judges rule, as in the very time of Moses; you are no longer required to place your hand on the Bible and swear to God. Of course, the world has made such a mess of just who God is anyway.

Matt. 5:37

But let your Yes be Yes and your No, No. For whatever is more than these is from the evil one.

Exod. 18: 21,22

Moreover you shall select from all the able men, such as fear God, men of truth, hating covetousness; and place such over them to be rulers ....

And let them judge the people at all times ....

So now, if any moral compass is removed, just how do you trust the testimony?

It's all up to man's great wisdom I guess? I say that with tongue in cheek as I know all true Wisdom is from God.

Prov. 9:10

The fear of the Lord is the beginning of wisdom, and the knowledge of the Holy One is understanding.

When I read my Bible I always gravitate to the words of Jesus written in red.

Matt. 5:17,18,19

Do not think that I came to destroy the Law or the prophets. I did not come to destroy but fulfill.

For assuredly, I say to you, till heaven and earth pass away, one jot or one title will by no means pass from the Law till all is fulfilled.

Whoever therefore breaks one of the least of these commandments, and teaches men so, shall be called least in the Kingdom of heaven; but whoever does and teaches them, he shall be called great in the Kingdom of heaven.

And in conclusion ………

Eccl. 12:13
Let us hear the conclusion of the whole matter.

Fear God and keep His commandments,

For this is man's all.

Let's Try Here

I'm afraid this is another ouch chapter for most of us.

Exod. 20:8
Remember the Sabbath day to keep it holy.

Okay where are we on this one Church?

We can blame the government in this 21st century for allowing businesses to be open on our chosen Sabbath or Sunday, however; we can't blame them that we should choose to work, plough fields, or go shopping in the stores that have chosen to stay open.

God is not demanding that we go to church on the Sabbath. Jesus did establish His church and it is the obvious place to worship God, but that is not the original meaning to Sabbath. Nor is God asking us to give up family and fun.

God is asking us to rest on the seventh day just as He did after creation. He rested and saw that all was good. We must return to the Sabbath rest and see that all is good that comes from God. Give Him the thanks and praise that He deserves. Life does work with one day completely set aside for rest. It is only in the very shortest time of history that this has changed.

It is one of God's commandments write at the top of the list. Have you ever thought; how could the Israelite's have danced around an idol of gold while Moses was on the mountain with God when the Commandments were being written? Have you ever thought to yourself; I'm a good Christian I go to church on Sunday? Do you keep the Sabbath? The Sabbath is clearly a day of rest from work; even your employees; even if they are not Christian. Really think about this one. If you take the day to go shopping, are you forcing the shop keeper to remain open?

I like this Quaker tradition of the inner light:

There is that of God in every person; and that of God in everything.

We know the first commandment is to love God with all your heart; soul; and strength. If God is truly first in your life you will indeed want to give Him first place in your day of rest. If you have given yourself to Him, He recognises you as His child. For myself as a mother, there is nothing that makes me happier than when my children are all around me. Family together, enjoying each other and all the great things God has given us will bring great rest and joy. Go fishing, play ball whatever, it is in the act of the Sabbath day that counts.

Isa. 58: 13, 14

If you turn your foot from the Sabbath, from doing your pleasure on My holy day, And call the Sabbath a delight, The holy day of the Lord honorable, And shall honor Him, not doing your own ways, Nor finding your own pleasure, Nor speaking your own words,

Then you shall delight yourself in the Lord; And I will cause you to ride on the high hills of the earth, And feed you with the heritage of Jacob your father.

The mouth of the Lord has spoken.

We don't need to be extremists here, but we can't blame the government, or society how we use or don't use the Sabbath any more than we can blame the government for legalising abortion. It is always our choice. Free Will!

Here are a couple of verses from Nehemiah 13 to chew on.

Neh. 13: 15, 17, 18

In those days saw I in Judah some treading wine presses on the Sabbath, and bringing in sheaves, and loading asses; as also wine, grapes, and figs, and all manner of burdens, which they brought into Jerusalem on the Sabbath day; and I testified against them in the day wherein they sold victuals.

Then I contended with the nobles of Judah and said unto them, what evil thing is this that you do, and profane the Sabbath day?

Did not your father's thus, and did not our God bring all this evil upon us, and upon this city? Yet you bring more wrath upon Israel by profaning the Sabbath.

Now I want to tell you a true story of much more recent history. The story was told by a priest and there is unexplainable physical evidence to back up the story. When my children were young we made a roadside stop at a small shrine in rural Quebec during one summer holiday. The shrine is maintained as a reminder of the mysterious incident that occurred there in the 1800's.

As the story goes a farmer had a field which the local priest had to pass each Sunday morning on his way to church. The farmer's wife attended the Sunday mass and would give excuses to the priest for her husband who would not attend. Each and every Sunday the priest would take the opportunity to invite the farmer to church, always having his plea ignored. One Sunday morning the farmer had his horse and a wagon working in the field as the priest came by and pleaded with the man one more time to join him at church. As usual his invite was rejected. It was on the priests return past the farmer's field that the story reaches its magnitude. There was no farmer in the field, nor horse, nor wagon but a field filled to great depths of rounded large stones that baffles geologists to this day. The farmer, his horse, nor his wagon were ever found. Nothing will grow in this perfect field of stone although lush vegetation and trees have now surrounded it. It is a very mystical place to visit indeed.

I would like to leave this chapter with some profound words of Andrew Bonar that pierced me to the heart.

> *It is not the importance of the thing, but the majesty of the Lawgiver, that is to be the standard of obedience ...*

He went on to say; the principle involved in obedience or disobedience was none other than the same principle which was tried in the Garden of Eden at the foot of the forbidden tree.

It is really this:

> *Is the Lord to be obeyed in all things whatsoever He commands? Is He a holy Lawgiver? Are His creatures bound to give implicit assent to His will?*

Acts 17: 30, 31

Truly, these times of ignorance God overlooked, but now commands all men everywhere to repent

Because He has appointed a day on which He will judge the world in righteousness by the Man Whom He has ordained. He has given assurance of this to all by raising Him from the dead.

Divided You Fall

Now after the flood Noah lived 950 years and was the father of many nations. The whole earth had one language and one speech. It came to pass, as they journeyed from the east they settled in the plain of Shinar. They decided to build a great city and a tower to heaven to make a name for themselves. And so they did, but the Lord came down to see what they had done.

> **Gen. 11:6**
> *And the Lord said," Indeed the people are one and they have one language, and this is what they begin to do; now nothing they propose to do will be withheld from them".*

I want you to see that together they were able to build a tower to heaven and that God Himself said that nothing they proposed to do would be withheld from them. It was pride that brought the tower down.

Jesus Himself said that a house divided falls.

> **Matt. 12:25**
> *But Jesus knew their thoughts and said to them: every Kingdom divided against itself is brought to desolation, and every city or house divided against itself will not stand.*

Come on Church, we are all in God's Kingdom, a Kingdom severely divided.

Noah's descendants together built a tower to the heavens. Once they stopped speaking the same language they had no power at all.

Sure, our churches have the occasional united prayer service and the even less frequent get together but we need to get radical in these times before Jesus returns. We need to tear down the walls of our religion and become one undivided Kingdom united in Christ Jesus.

Eph. 4:14,15
That we should no longer be children, tossed to and fro and carried about with every wind of doctrine, by the trickery of men, in the cunning craftiness of deceitful plotting,

But, speaking the truth in love, may grow up in all things into Him who is the head- Christ-

It's time to get real with our Faith.
It's time to re-build God's temple.
It's time to follow Jesus.

Have we forgotten we belong to God, and that only His word reigns supreme? Do we include God in our daily walk as Adam and Eve did? Religion has become nothing more than rules and regulations and membership tied up in religious pride. Hey folks; I am not condemning church here! It's just that our churches need to look the way Jesus intended them. We the body of Christ are church.

Eph. 1: 17, 18, 19

That the God of our Lord Jesus Christ, the Father of glory, may give to you the Spirit of wisdom and revelation in the knowledge of Him

The eyes of your understanding being enlightened that you may know what is the hope of His calling, what are the riches of the glory of His inheritance in the saints

And what is the exceeding greatness of His power towards us who believe according to the working of His mighty power

We are all God's children and we can all receive the Holy Spirit and hear directly from God. It's in His word.

1 Cor. 2: 14,15

But the natural man does not receive the things of the Spirit of God, for they are foolishness to him; nor can he know them, because they are spiritually discerned.

But he who is spiritual judges all things, yet he himself is rightly judged by no one.

King David was a shepherd boy who talked with God long before he became a great King.

Jesus did not die so that we could have religion, but that through His covering, we could return to a personal relationship with His Father, our Father.

Eph. 4:5

One Lord, one faith, one baptism;

The Church has taken the beautiful, uncomplicated message of Christ, and turned it into a complicated multiple choice, set of rules that sets its brothers and sisters at odds. Satan doesn't have to come against the church, our endless number of denominations and differences do it for him.

We must assume some of the blame for our churches. In this Me generation we want to pick and choose our brand or flavor of church. We go about looking for a church kind of like Goldie Locks and the 3 bears. So, to accommodate our varied tastes the church has watered down the message of God. After all they wouldn't want to offend anyone or have them leave the church. Lots of activities, babysitting perhaps; whatever it takes but go easy on the sins.

Church! Unite! In love and in Jesus.

How is it that the Islamists or Buddhists have learned this unity so well? Their strength comes from their unity.

Church how can we bring people to Christ with all our rules and legalisms? How can we bring people to Christ with all our differences and disagreements?

The law kills and the Spirit gives life. If Jesus is in us we bring Him to church and not the other way around.

1 Cor. 12:7
But the manifestation of the Spirit is given to each one for the profit of all

We need one church just as there is only one God and one way to God through Jesus Christ. Can we become a Christian Church and nothing else?

Phil. 2:2
Fulfill my joy by being like-minded, having the same love, being of one accord, of one mind

It is time for us to unite as one Christian army, to come against our real enemy. We must unite in the cross of Jesus and embrace our differences.

1 Tim.2:4
No one engaged in warfare entangles himself with the affairs of this life, that he may please him who enlisted him as a soldier.

7 Warnings

Rev. 2:7

He who has an ear let him hear what the Spirit says to the churches. To him who overcomes I will give to eat from the tree of life, which is in the midst of the Paradise of God

Wow! Could it be that the very tree humanity was banished from the Garden for, God will give us to eat from? Let the magnitude of that sink in for a minute. God forbid us to take from the tree of knowledge in the Garden, but He will freely give it through His Spirit.

It does not matter who the 7 churches are in the Book of Revelations but most importantly what the warnings are to the church and who is to be found guilty.

Ephesus: Return to your first love – Jesus

Rev. 2: 4,5

"Nevertheless I have this against you, that you have left your first love.

"Remember therefore from where you have fallen; repent and do the first works, or else I will come to you quickly and remove your lampstand from it's place unless you repent.

7 Warnings

Smyrna: Hold fast to your Faith under pressure

Rev. 2:10

"Do not fear any of those things which you are about to suffer. Indeed, the devil is about to throw some of you into prison, that you may be tested, and you will have tribulation days. Be faithful unto death, and I will give you the crown of life.

Pegamos: Don't let life seduce you from your Faith.

Rev. 2:14

But I have a few things against you, because you have there those who hold the doctrine of Balaam who taught Balak to put a stumbling block before the children of Israel to eat things sacrificed to idols, and to commit sexual immorality.

Thyatira: Sins of the flesh – that old self wants what it wants.

Rev. 2: 20,23

Nevertheless I have a few things against you, because you allow that woman Jezebel, who calls herself a prophetess to teach and seduce My servants to commit sexual immorality and eat things sacrificed to idols.

"I will kill her children with death, and all the churches shall know that I Am He who searches the minds and hearts. And I will give to each one of you according to your works."

Sardis: God does not want you works but your true Worship.

Rev. 3: 1,2,3

"And to the angel of the church in Sardis write; "These things says He who has the seven Spirits of God and the seven stars: "I know your works, that you have a name that you are alive, but you are dead.

Be watchful and strengthen the things which remain, that are ready to die, for I have not found your works perfect before God.

Remember therefore how you have received and heard; holdfast and repent. Therefore if you will not watch, I will come upon you as a thief and you will not know what hour I will come upon you.

Gal. 3:3

Are you so foolish? Having begun in the Spirit, are you now being made perfect by the flesh?

Philadelphia: Hold on tight little flock.

Rev. 3:10,11

"Because you have kept My command to persevere, I also will keep you from the hour of trial which shall come upon the whole world, to test those who dwell on the earth.

Behold, I Am coming quickly! Hold fast what you have, that no one may take your crown.

Laodiceans: Where is your Holy Ghost fire?

Rev. 3: 15, 16, 17

I know your works, that you are neither cold nor hot. I could wish that you were cold or hot.

So then because you are lukewarm, neither cold nor hot, I will vomit you out of my mouth.

"Because you say I am rich, have become wealthy and have need of nothing"- and do not know that you are wretched, miserable, poor, blind and naked.

Heb. 3:7 – 10

Therefore, as the Holy Spirit says: "Today if you will hear His voice,

Do not harden your hearts as in the rebellion, in the day of trial in the wilderness,

Where your fathers tested Me, tried Me, and saw My works for forty years.

Therefore I was angry with that generation, and said, "They always go astray in their heart, and they have not known My ways."

All of the warnings are to us the body of Christ, His church?

The spirit of the Antichrist is already in the church.

1 John 2:18

Little children, it is the last hour; and as you have heard that the Antichrist is coming, even now many antichrists have come, by which we know that it is the last hour.

Contrary

There has been a common theme through this book, which considers the fact that we live so contrary or backwards to the will of God; to the way Jesus has taught us.

John 3: 11,12
This is the message you heard from the beginning. We should love one another. Do not be like Cain who belonged to the evil one and murdered his brother.

And this is how we know what love is; Jesus Christ laid down His life for us, and we ought to lay down our lives for our brothers and sisters.

I would like to present here how the religion of Islam is the exact opposite to Christianity.

Did you know that a Mosque now sits on God's temple Mount?

2 Thess. 2: 4,11
Who opposes and exalts himself above all that is called God or that is worshipped, so that he sits as God in the Temple of God, showing himself that he is God?

And for this reason God will send them strong delusion, that they should believe the lie.

Islam	Christianity
Demands believers convert	Free will. ***Gal. 5:1*** *Stand fast therefore in the liberty by which Christ has made us free, and do not be entangled again with a yoke of bondage.*
Fight for Allah	God will fight for us. ***Eph. 6:10*** *Finally, my brethren, be strong in the Lord and in the power of His might.*
Requires revenge	Love your enemies. ***Matt. 5:44*** *"But I say to you, love your enemies, bless those who curse you, do good to those who hate you, and pray for those who spitefully use you and persecute you,"*
Allah is remote to believers	God came to us. ***John 3:16*** *For God so love the world that He gave His only begotten Son, that whoever believes in Him should not perish but have everlasting life.*

Islam	Christianity
Allah condemns	Jesus does not. ***John 3:17*** *"For God did not send His Son into the world to condemn the world, but that the world through Him might be saved.*
Allah brings great fear of punishment	Giver of love only. ***Isa. 41:10*** *Fear not, for I am with you; be not dismayed for I am your God. I will strengthen you, yes I will help you, I will uphold you with My righteous right hand.*
Die for Allah and go to heaven	God died for us ***John 3:16***

We must never forget that our Savior gave His life, for us and never try to earn Heaven for ourselves.

John 15:15
I no longer call you servants because a servant does not know his master's business. Instead I have called you friends for everything that I learned from My Father I have made known to you.

The God of the Jews, our God, is painted for us through Jewish history, lacking the grace of Jesus but demonstrating the love of God. The Muslim God, portrayed by the prophet Mohammed is lacking the grace of Jesus and is untrue of our God. Our God of today, the Christian God retains the Jewish history, is based on the grace of Jesus, but is often tainted by recent Christian history.

As history is all we have for our mind to comprehend, we must through our heart be taught and led by the Spirit of God to truly know God.

These Works

There are thousands of Christians in Church today, who are overworked and in an underfed condition. Many Christians who desire a strong relationship with God, have followed all the church rules and yet find themselves tired and empty. In desiring to please God, they have replaced seeking God with working for Him.

Much has been written about the Saints, often hundreds of years after their great works and miracles. The part of the Saints life that is usually skipped over is the fact that these great Saints spent most of their time in solitude and in a deep personal relationship with Jesus. They didn't get to be Saints through their church association or activity. St. Francis in fact struggled for permission from the church to go off to solitude and begin his ministry. Some Saints were confined to their bed and did not even attend church.

> **Luke 10: 40 -42**
>
> But Martha was distracted with much serving, and she approached Him and said, "Lord, do you not care that my sister has left me to serve alone? Therefore, tell her to help me."
>
> And Jesus answered and said to her; "Martha, Martha, you are worried and troubled about many things.

But one thing is needed, and Mary has chosen that good part, which will not be taken away from her."

Catholics please don't throw down this book, but if you study Martin Luther, you will discover that he had a strong desire to give the scriptures and Jesus back to the people. The Catholic Church at the time had decided that it's people could not understand the scriptures and so much of it was burned or locked away to keep them from error. Albeit the people were largely uneducated and poor, they were also presumed to not be able to hear from God themselves.

Psalm 40: 6, 7, 8   A Psalm of David
Sacrifice and offering You did not desire; my ears you have opened. Burnt offering and sin offering You did not require.

Then I said, "Behold I come; in the scroll of the book it is written of me.

I delight to do Your will, O my God, and Your law is within my heart."

Many Christians today are living under the Old Testament Law and are missing out on the blessings of the New Testament Grace of Jesus. We are called to relationship with Jesus, not to religious activity devoid of the relationship. It just can't work without the relationship.

Rev. 3: 7, 8
And to the angel of the church in Philadelphia write, "These things says He who is Holy, He who is true, He

who has the Key of David, He who opens and no one shuts, and shuts an no one opens:

I know your works. See I have set before you an open door, and no one can shut it; for you have a little strength, have kept My word, and have not denied My name."

Eph. 2:8,9
For by grace you have been saved through faith and that not of yourselves; it is the gift of God,

Not of works, lest anyone should boast.

I must write of a painful conviction I received in my spirit concerning a Catholic teaching that I had practised. Catholics are taught to pray for dead souls, and especially those in purgatory. My search to find purgatory in the scriptures, all the while praying to God for direction, led to my frightening conviction. I had believed that my prayers could actually save souls in purgatory and in this belief Satan had deceived me greatly into a prideful ritual. The realization in my spirit that I had believed I could save them! Does Jesus not judge where we will go and is He not a fair judge? First conviction.

Luke 16:25,26
"But Abraham said, "Son remember that in your lifetime you received good things, and likewise Lazarus evil things; but now he is comforted and you are tormented.

"And besides all this, between us and you a great gulf is fixed, so that those who want to pass from here to you cannot, nor can those from there pass to us."

My spirit was sorrowful, as I had believed that our Father God would condemn anyone to a purgatory, when I could clearly find no record of purgatory in the scriptures, but worse my shameful pride that my prayers could overturn God's decisions.

Rev. 20:12
And I saw the dead, small and great, standing before God, and books were opened. And another book was opened, which is the Book of Life. And the dead were judged according to their works, by the things that were written in the books.

Scripture is clear on our judgement and whether we are written in the Lambs Book of Life. Scripture is also very clear that our chance for redemption is during our lifetime. Prayers are needed for the living alone.

Luke 16: 28,29
"for I have five brothers, that he may testify to them, lest they also come to this place of torment."

"Abraham said to him, They have Moses and the Prophets; let them hear them."

I must confess that this practice of praying for the dead now seems foolish to me. If our loved one has gone home to be with Jesus, do we really think they need our prayers? They have either received their glory in Heaven, or not! Do we presume our prayers will what? – Change the outcome. Just asking?

Luke 20:37,38

"But even Moses showed in the burning bush passage that the dead are raised, when he called the Lord "the God of Abraham, the God of Isaac, and the God of Jacob."

"For He is not the God of the dead but of the living, for all live to Him."

No need to be discouraged here. See the power in your prayers to save someone from hell while they are still living." You have the power" as they say, His name is Jesus. Dwell on the words of Jesus. You have not because you ask not.

Luke 11:9

"So I say to you, ask, and it will be given to you; seek, and you will find; knock, and it will be opened to you.

Peace?

Political peace is deceptive peace. In 1938 Adolf Hitler signed the Munich Agreement as a promise of peace. In 1939 Hitler invaded Poland and the Second World War began.

In the 21st century we have become escape artists from reality. We numb ourselves from what's happening in the world through movies, T.V., internet and even isolated destination vacations (to escape our smart phones which we can't leave behind). Where is the peace?

Islam claims theirs is a religion of peace but we have read in the previous chapter how this is contrary to the truth.

Jesus came into the world to bring peace. This is the peace that the angel announced at Jesus birth and that He exemplified with His life. Divine peace that you feel inside when the world is falling apart; peace with your neighbour, with your Christian brothers and sisters.

Luke 2:14
Glory to God in the highest, and on earth peace, goodwill toward men!

This is the peace that non-believers cannot comprehend.

Phil. 4:7

And the peace of God, that surpasses all understanding, will guard your hearts and minds through Christ Jesus.

John 16:33

"These things I have spoken to you, that in Me you may have peace. In the world you will have tribulation, but be of good cheer, I have overcome the world."

This is the same peace that we should demonstrate as Christians especially when all the signs seem to be pointing to the end times.

John 14:27

Jesus said:

"Peace I leave with you; My peace I give you. I do not give to you as the world gives. Do not let your hearts be troubled and do not be afraid.

Rev. 14:2

Hear is the patience of the saints; here are those who keep the Commandments of God and the faith of Jesus.

Jesus is referred to in scripture as the prince of peace. He is also called the Morning star which I find rather ironic for the Jewish nation who carries His star on their flag.

I Come Quickly

Rev. 22:12
"and behold I am coming quickly, and My reward is with Me, to give to everyone according to his work.

The truth as laid out in scripture is that Jesus will return. Since the time of Jesus resurrection, we have ben expecting His return. Jesus said that no man knows the time or hour, but that we must be ready. We know He will return at the end of the time of the gentiles and we seem to have no problem believing this truth in all the different Christian denominations. Perhaps we easily submit to this belief because it demands nothing from us.

On the other hand, the rest of scripture does require commitment from us. First and foremost is the complete surrendering of our will to God's. By far the most difficult part of our life's journey.

If you read the dictionary description of surrender, it becomes apparent why it is so difficult for us.

Surrender
- to give up possession of or power over; yield to another on demand or compulsion

- to give up claim to; give over or yield, esp. voluntarily as in favor of another

- to give up or abandon (surrendering all hope)

- to yield or resign oneself to an emotion, influence etc.

- to give oneself up to another's power or control, especially as a prisoner

… and on and on.

This above very long description of surrender reminds me of just how much we have burdened and confused what it means to be Christian.

Regardless of how you have worked out your own personal definition as a believer, one thing is certain. When our Lord returns His timing will be sudden and unexpected.

Matt. 24:27
"For as the lightning comes from the east and flashes to the west, so also will the coming of the Son of man be.

Live each day with urgency and expectancy. This daily battle we face, whether it is sickness or Islamic extremists, is not a battle against flesh and blood but against spiritual forces.

Eph. 6:12
For we do not wrestle against flesh and blood but against principalities, against powers, against the rulers of darkness of this age, against spiritual hosts of wickedness in the heavenly places.

Time lines in scripture are not actually of the earth but rather of Gods spiritual realm. Jesus has been protecting us against the evil spiritual realm since we were created. Jesus explains to Daniel what has been happening in the spiritual realm to Israel as well as what is to come in the spiritual realm in the end times.

Dan. 10:20
Do you know why I have come to you? And now I must return to fight with the prince of Persia; and when I have gone forth indeed the Prince of Greece will come.

There is striking repetition of Daniel's revelations of the end of days and that of John's so called End Time prophecies. They are both given as warnings as to mankind's reward if they do not return to God. The timelines and events unfold according to God's timing which is kept secret from man. We must realize that places and timelines are all of the spiritual realm which in turn affects our time lines and not the other way around.

Rev. 9:11
And they had over them the angel of the bottomless pit, whose name in Hebrew is Abaddon, but in Greek he has the name Apollyon.

Rev. 11:8
And their dead bodies will lie in the street of the great city which spiritually is called Sodom and Egypt, where also the Lord was crucified.

Rev. 17:17
"For God has put it into their hearts to fulfill His purpose, to be of one mind, and to give their Kingdom to the beast, until the words of God are fulfilled.

The scriptures are full of supernatural messengers.

Mal. 3:1
"Behold, I send My messenger, and he will prepare the way before Me. And the Lord, whom you seek, will suddenly come to His temple, even the messenger of the covenant, in whom you delight. Behold, He is coming, says the Lord of hosts.

Extreme weather and world events foretold in the scriptures, all seem to be flashing like warning signs, but sadly at this time of the world there are so few Christians and even fewer who believe that Jesus is returning soon.

Jesus first coming has been written of and painted as a most beautiful scene with stars and angels, glorious singing and our Savior is born. Jesus second coming not so pretty and certainly not celebrated.

Why not? Why do we fear the tribulations and world events? We have never been left without the answer. Only one answer – Jesus-

Rom. 8:9
But you are not in the flesh but in the spirit, if indeed the Spirit of God dwells in you. Now if anyone does not have the Spirit of Christ, he is not His.

It doesn't matter whether you can figure out end time prophecy but have you figured out your own relationship with Jesus?

Ezek. 33:31
"So they come to you as people do, they sit before you as My people, and they hear your words, but they do not do them; for with their mouth they show much love, but their hearts pursue their own gain."

Prophecy

There has been so much written about end time prophecy and yes I admit I have read a great deal of it; but we have gotten so bogged down trying to figure out timelines and events that we have missed the whole point. It doesn't matter about the who and when, but the greater question is have you figured out if you are going to heaven?

Prophets and prophecy were given to firstly warn us of the consequences of our deadly sinful ways and secondly so we would have time to repent from those ways before our time is up. Each wave of intense evil has had had its share of prophets to warn and to save, but we have been given the Savior Himself. Are we listening?

> ***2 Peter 1:19,20,21***
> *And so we have the prophetic word confirmed, which you do well to heed as a light that shines in a dark place, until the day dawns and the morning star rises in your hearts,*
>
> *Knowing this first, that no prophecy of Scripture is of any private interpretation*
>
> *For prophecy never came by the will of man, but holy men of God spoke as they were moved by the Holy Spirit.*

Gen. 6:30

And the Lord said "My Spirit shall not strive with man forever; for he is indeed flesh.

Let's take a step back to just a few of the prophets.

2 Peter 2: 4,5,6,7

For God did not spare the angels who sinned, but cast them down to hell and delivered them into chains of darkness, to be reserved for judgement;

And did not spare the ancient world, but saved Noah, one of eight people, a preacher of righteousness bringing in the flood on the world of the ungodly;

And turning the cities of Sodom and Gomorrah into ashes condemned them to destruction, making them an example to those who afterward would live ungodly;

Isa. 50:10

"Who among you fears the Lord? Who obeys the voice of His servant? Who walks in darkness and has no light? Let him trust in the name of the Lord and rely upon His God.

John the Baptist our last and scripture says, our greatest prophet, went about announcing the coming of our redemption.

Matt. 3:3

For this is he who was spoken of by the prophet Isaiah, saying: The voice of one crying in the wilderness: prepare the way of the Lord; make His paths straight.

Now let us look to our saving Grace, sent to us by our Father Himself.

Luke 2:10, 11
Then the angel said to them, "Do not be afraid, for behold, I bring you glad tidings of great joy which will be to all people.

"For there is born to you this day in the city of David a Savior who is Christ the Lord.

Why should we have any fear of the second coming of Jesus? Do we doubt God's word, or do we doubt our own belief? The scriptures are not just words but life.

2 Peter 3: 2,7
That you may be mindful of the words which were spoken before by the holy prophets, and of the commandment of us the apostles of the Lord our Savior,

But the heavens and the earth which are now preserved by the same words are reserved for fire until the day of judgement and perdition of ungodly men.

Warning Lights

On our journey as a child of God, it is a grave mistake not to know and study the Old Testament scriptures; after all it is our history. We study history to advert similar mistakes of health, the environment and war. Why not scripture?

John 1:1
In the beginning was the Word, and the Word was with God, and the Word was God.

Scripture does not just contain the Word of God, it is God. Let that sink in for a minute. It is living, supernatural in origin, eternal in duration, infinite in scope and hand delivered from heaven.

It is Jesus guiding us through life just like a life coach. Think of your Bible as your Owner's Manual. If you had never owned a car before, you would have to thoroughly read your Owner's Manual to learn how to operate and maintain it. You would consult your manual at the slightest noise, vibration, or breakdown.

Well: you should consult the Scriptures (your Owner's Manual) for the slightest decision, difficulty or meltdown. If your car breaks down it can be fixed, and if you break down or have a breakdown you can be fixed too. However; just as you may ignore warning lights on the dashboard of your vehicle and it becomes seriously damaged, if you ignore the warnings in Scripture, you may become seriously damaged as well.

We do regular maintenance on our vehicles, because we can't prevent or fix what we are not aware of, but what of ourselves?

> **Matt. 4:4**
> *But He answered and said, "It is written, Man shall not live by bread alone, but by every word that proceeds from the mouth of God."*

God has been watching over and saving His people since He created them. I've heard Christians espouse that such a loving God would never allow or bring disaster upon His people. Well they are right and they are wrong.

God does not bring things upon people (save for blessings), but people ignore the warnings and bring it upon themselves. Think about every great disaster upon mankind and note how desperately and for how long God pleaded with them to turn from their ways.

You already know how long Noah pleaded with people to make ready to get into his Ark. Abraham pleaded with God not to destroy Sodom and Gomorrah if there could be found any righteous men.

> **Gen. 18: 32**
> *Then he said, let not the Lord be angry, and I will speak but once more; suppose ten should be found there? And He said, "I will not destroy it for the sake of ten."*

Moses pleaded with Pharaoh to let Gods chosen people go. God through Moses brought several disasters upon Pharaoh and his people as a warning of God's might. Pharaoh had hardened his heart until ultimately God took his firstborn son along with all the first born sons of Egypt.

Now I believe there is another foolish thing that we say of God. How often have you heard; thankfully the Lord took them home to spare them the pain?

1 Peter 5:8
Be sober; be vigilant; because your adversary the devil walks about like a roaring lion, seeking whom he may devour

This whole relatively new path that mankind has been sliding down, regarding legalised abortion; removing life support; legalised assisted suicide and ultimately letting doctors decide who lives and who dies is oh so dangerous.

Who is deciding when you are ready for heaven?

Has God been trying to warn us of our slippery slide downwards?

Many books have been written to warn mankind of it's deadly nature, but ultimately the warnings are imbedded in scripture. Let's not become another global warning (not warming) and disaster story for history. Please; just get into God's word for yourself; please! It would seem that the Scriptures have become no more than X files; hidden away, buried in the dark; kept from the public, only to be discovered by a few inquisitive souls.

There is on television wright now a series called Vikings. It is written as a historical view of a brutal race, conquering and murdering their way through the northern world. They are portrayed as believing in many gods, but to be unaware of our God and Jesus Christ. The writers want you to like these murdering characters by justifying their behavior because they are heathens after all.

When our history is written, what will be our excuse for killing babies, the sick, and the elderly? Sorry those words pain me as much as you.

How's Your Receiver?

The Scriptures tell us, that Jesus and His disciples went about preaching, teaching and healing. They often held large outdoor healing services. Those who hold healing services today are often labelled extremists.

Act. 10:38
"How God anointed Jesus of Nazareth with the Holy Spirit and with power, who went about doing good and healing all who were oppressed by the devil, for God was with Him.

Where did we get the idea that healing only pertained to Jesus time? I have a pretty good idea. ssss

John 14:12
Most assuredly; I say to you, he who believes in Me, the works that I do he will do also; and greater works than these he will do because I go to My Father.

I believe Jesus was pretty clear in the above verse, that we should be asking and believing for healing of any and all sickness or disease. Why be a Christian if you don't want to receive what God wants to give you? In true God fashion, the more you believe the more you receive. We must fine tune our receiver to get in the flow of blessings that God has waiting for each of us.

I'd like to bring attention again where scripture says that Jesus healed all who were oppressed by the devil.

I suppose a talk about exorcism is way out there for you?

Eph. 6:11,12
Put on the whole armor of God, that you may be able to stand against the wiles of the devil.

For we do not wrestle against flesh and blood, but against principalities, against powers, against the rulers of the darkness of this age, against spiritual hosts of wickedness in the heavenly places.

I had a very dear friend Father Jim, who has gone home to be with the Lord, and who was one of the last Catholic exorcists in Canada. The Catholic Church, who once ordained exorcists, has now decided that the process is much too controversial.

Father Jim used to share hair raising stories concerning a Jewish woman whom he was helping convert to Christianity. Sorry I have to interrupt the programming here because just typing Father Jim raises an issue that convicts me each time I say or write it.

Matt. 23:9
"Do not call anyone on earth your father; for One is your Father, He who is in heaven."

Okay on with the story. Now Father Jim met with this woman regularly in her kitchen. He said that at times when he left her kitchen it looked like a bomb had gone off. Tables, chairs, cupboards and cutlery would fly at him. She did successfully go on to become a Christian thanks to the courage and strong belief of Father Jim. I repeat this story simply to remind you that the scriptures do warn us.

1 Peter 5:8
Be sober; be vigilant; because your adversary the devil walks about like a roaring lion, seeking whom he may devour.

I personally have had many supernatural experiences and I will include a few here only to point to scripture.

Many years ago, while praying in a tiny Chapel, enjoying the presence of the Lord, I foolishly asked God; "If I could carry some of His pain and suffering". Well! According to my good friend and retired Doctor sitting beside me, I slumped down in my seat lifeless for a brief moment. Not to worry I instantly recuperated; but this is what Jesus said to me: "O child I only let you experience but a grain of sand on a vast beach of suffering and pain" it is all your human heart could bare.

Luke 24:25,26
Then He said to them, "O foolish ones, and slow of heart to believe in all that the prophets have spoken!

"Ought not the Christ to have suffered these things and to enter into His glory?

I do not tell the next story to frighten you, but to tell you of the peace I received from knowing that I am surrounded by divine protection. One day upon leaving a noonday Mass at the Cathedral; as I stepped off the last step, the sidewalk became a thick black pool of creatures before my eyes. To my surprise I did not fall into but walked upon the creatures in complete protection from them. I was also aware of creatures on the hydro wires, crackling like the birds from the Alfred Hitchcock movie. When I reached the corner, everything returned back to normal. What could have been a terrifying experience became a great comfort for me, knowing that nothing I had seen could touch me.

Prov. 1:33
But whoever listens to me will dwell safely, And will be secure without fear of evil."

Now I am going to tell you of my most treasured spiritual experience. In the 1990's I took part in a" Life in the Spirit" seminar given at our Catholic church. Before each weekly session we would participate in Mass. After receiving communion at one of these Mass's I was kneeling and complaining to myself how lifeless the large crucifix appeared to me. Suddenly my attention was drawn to the left and I marveled at a pair of feet in leather sandals. My eyes took their time to soak in every detail as they slowly drew upwards. I could not clearly see His face as He was so brilliantly back lit, but the countenance of Jesus is burned into my memory. His garment was of such brilliance and so finely woven. He gave me personal messages for certain people in attendance as he walked to each one and then walked to the alter and was gone. I am not sure why I was blessed to be able to see Him, although it was certainly not for any personal gratification. I have believed that my ability to perceive Jesus in the Spiritual realm was because of my recent baptism of the Holy Spirit.

John 3:3
Jesus answered and said to him, "Most assuredly, I say to you, unless one is born again, he cannot see the Kingdom of God."

My final story is both personal and miraculous. It is a story that could one day touch all of us. A family member and daughter of God suffered in her later years and finished her journey in the hospital on life support. Her family were summoned by the doctor and given the whole litany of what would happen when she was taken off of life support. The doctor conveyed that most patients pass within the day however the maximum would be 3 days. Well this child of God lived over two weeks, much to the anguish of the doctor, as all fluids had been ordered withdrawn from her. What does her death say to us? I don't know, but I do know the One and Only who does. I know she had long ago surrendered her will and her life to Him and that she would only go when He had ordered it.

As I am recalling this emotional part of my journey, I find myself disturbed over this greatest final decision of life; perhaps one that we will have no control over. Who have we assigned over our final wishes? Have we asked a true believer to be in control of our deteriorating health, and can we be certain they will still be a believer when our time has arrived? We will never know if our last wishes will be carried out, argued in court, or lost in the confusion, or if the Doctor giving sentence is a believer. Truly this is something we should pray about concerning the last steps of our journey.

Very few believers ever experience the supernatural. How unfortunate that when death is so close and heaven so near, that some report seeing their loved ones and Jesus.

Mark 16:17,18
"And these signs will follow those who believe: in My name they will cast out demons; they will speak with new tongues;

They will take up serpents; and if they drink anything deadly, it will by no means hurt them; they will lay hands on the sick and they will recover."

I am going to talk about praying in tongues here, because it is often put in the spooky category. Speaking in tongues does not belong to the Evangelical or Pentecostal faith alone. It is the language of heaven, required to penetrate the throne room of God. Speaking in tongues is like having the Holy Spirit as our personal translator. God knows what we need above anything we could ask for.

Healing as well has often been relegated to the way out there; Evangelical; special few, category. As scripture says, it is for all who believe.

Healing in the name of Jesus or casting out demons is a two-way system, just as we exist in two realms. The believer calling on the name of Jesus enters the spiritual realm, where the demon or sickness exists but faith is and always was the trigger to call the healing into our realm. Once again, there is a two-way system that must happen to receive our healing. The one calling upon Jesus must believe Jesus gave us His name and power to use and the one being healed must not only believe that Jesus secured our healing on the cross, but believe that they have been made worthy to receive their healing through their faith in Jesus Christ.

If our receiver is jammed in any way, Jesus cannot get our healing to us. Our biggest blockage to receiving our healing from Jesus seems to lie in the fact that we feel unworthy. Sorry, but that is actually thinking more highly of yourself and forgetting the huge sacrifice Jesus died to give us.

Nothing you can do; nothing you have done; nothing you will do will keep Him from loving you.

Get over yourself!

He loves you!

He loved you first!

Peter 2:24

Who Himself bore our sins in His own body on the tree, that we, having died to sins, might live for righteousness – by whose stripes you were healed.

John 15:16

"you did not choose Me, but I chose you and appointed you that you should bear fruit, and that your fruit should remain, that whatever you ask the Father in My Name He may give you."

Don't ask me why but I feel the need to add this message here. I don't argue with the Lord.

As having been a Catholic and now a non-denominational Christian, I was surprised by the difference in the belief that Jesus had brothers and sisters on earth. Catholics no and Protestants yes. You should be aware that in the Hebrew language there is no word for cousin. They refer to their cousins as brothers and sisters.

Luke 8:21
But He answered and said to them, "My mother and My brothers are those who hear the word of God and do it

It's So Easy

1 Peter 5:7
Casting all your care upon Him, for He cares for you

I just love the following definition of worry.
"To torment oneself with disturbing thoughts"

I must admit this process of trusting God has been the most challenging for me. I grew up with the champion worrier, my mother. If anyone was five minutes late, she had them lying in a ditch somewhere half dead. She definitely knew God but she never entertained the thought to pray for that person. She was probably never taught that either.

Jesus Himself in Matthew 6 goes on for some length admonishing us not to worry about anything. Not what to wear, what to eat or drink and so on. He goes on to say that after all your heavenly Father knows that you need all these things

As Joyce Meyers always says: "Let go and let God"

Rev. 14:12
Here is the patience of the saints; here are those who keep the commandments of God and the faith of Jesus.

Turn your worry into prayer!
This whole worry business is tied to trust.

Prov. 3:5

Trust in the Lord with all your heart and lean not on your own understanding.

The above verse is a personal favorite of mine and the one which finally broke my vicious cycle of worry. I was always trying to fix or handle things on my own and I must admit I still struggle in this area.

Psalm 56:3,4

Whenever I am afraid, I will trust in You

In God (I will praise His word) In God I have put my trust;

I believe the whole trust issue has its roots in fear. Fear is the opposite of Faith. Fear would have you belong to the devil and faith to belong to God. Fear is crippling to both the soul and physical body. Faith is both freeing and healing to the body and soul. Fear's chains drag us to depths unimaginable while Faith frees our soul to soar beyond what we could ever dream.

The world is being crippled by fear. Even the non-waring countries of the United States, France, Germany and even my beloved Canada have experienced crippling fear. People and countries experiencing fear get smaller and smaller in stature. To remain in fear only continues the debilitating process. Satan knows this, why don't we.

I find it unfortunate that we have latched onto the term "Fear of the Lord". We are not actually told to fear God, but to fear not believing in Him and His word. We must fear that we do not love or reverence Him.

Prov. 1:7
The fear of the Lord is the beginning of knowledge, but fools despise wisdom and instruction.

It is ourselves that we should fear. Fear of not knowing God; fear of not knowing what the Scriptures contain.

They say that history repeats itself. From a historical perspective let's look at the Jewish nation. They were and are God's chosen and the first to receive God's written word. God gave them His laws in the form of a blessing or cursing and sent them many prophets when they veered off course.

Where is the Jewish nation at this time in history? They are scattered all over the world, as God said they would be, they are persecuted as God said they would be, and they missed their Savior.

It is not enough to read the Scriptures, but do you live them?

It is interesting to me that live backwards is evil. Let that one sink in.

Prov. 8:13
The fear of the Lord is to hate evil; pride and arrogance and the evil way and the perverse mouth I hate.

On a lighter note, I copied this poem out of our local newspaper written by anonymous.

Why Worry?

There are only two things to worry about. Either you are sick or you are well.

If you are well there is nothing to worry about. If you are sick, there are only two things to worry about.

Either you will get well, or die. If you get well there is nothing to worry about.

If you die, there are only two things to worry about. Either you will go to heaven or to hell.

If you go to heaven, there is nothing to worry about. If you go to hell, you'll be so damned busy shaking hands with all your friends you won't have time to worry.

Matt. 11:29
"Take My yoke upon you and learn from Me, for I am gentle and lowly in heart, and you will find rest for your souls.

You Choose

Deut. 30:19,20
I call heaven and earth as witnesses today against you, that I have set before you life and death, blessing and cursing; therefore choose life that both you and your descendants may live;

"that you may love the Lord your God, that you may obey His voice and that you may cling to Him, for He is your life and length of days; and that you may dwell in the land which the Lord swore to your fathers, to Abraham, Isaac, and Jacob, to give them."

I have always strived to teach my four children that life is about choices and consequences. I'm sure that they would tell you I was too strict and too religious. In fact, I have been accused of being too black and white and not allowing for any grey areas. I believe in wright and wrong according to God's word and nothing else.

I have always cringed at the word religious. I'm not religious. Jesus did not die so we could have religion but relationship. I am in a deep relationship with Jesus. I am perhaps in the latter years of my relationship with Jesus, but I continue to be more amazed, more in love each and every day.

We know that our manmade laws have consequences, and that breaking one of these laws will land you before a judge and final sentencing. God's laws work much the same way, although our sentencing does not come until death. The good news is that long before we come before our Judge for sentencing, we can reverse the outcome.

Isa. 66: 3,4
"He who kills a bull as if he slays a man; He who sacrifices a lamb, as if he breaks a dog's neck; He who offers a grain offering, as if he offers swine's blood; He who burns incense, as if he blesses an idol. Just as they have chosen their own ways, And their souls delight in their abominations,

So will I choose their delusions, And bring their fears on them; Because, when I called, no one answered, When I spoke they did not hear; But they did evil before My eyes, And chose that in which I do not delight."

Now I hope that in Deut. 30:20 you noticed that God said; you may obey His voice? We have all probably experienced that little voice in our head saying "just do it." I don't believe that was God's voice, but my point is that if the devil can plant thoughts in your head, do you not think that our great God can?

Folks we need to become deep Christians. Deep inner grounded Christians not surface, self centered earth surfers. Whoo I like that!

If you have a decision or choice to make, no matter how small or insignificant it may seem to you, God cares. Go to

God for the answer, it will make your life so much easier. Now the part that you may not like is that sometimes you have to wait for your answer. I know that we have become a people who hate to wait for anything.

Isa. 40:31
But those who wait on the Lord shall renew their strength; they shall mount up with wings like eagles, they shall run and not be weary, they shall walk and not faint.

I am going to be a little voice here and tell you to "just do it". I'm going to tell you again to trust the Lord.

I know I have just given you this scripture but I find it powerful as well as convicting.

Prov. 3:5
Trust in the Lord with all your heart, and lean not on your own understanding;

I am now approaching my 65th birthday and during a recent conversation with my oldest son Justin, he stated his surprise at how much my thinking had changed. My sobering thought was that it had taken me 65 years to change. Oh well, at least I had according to him. Our conversation was referencing the fact that our new Prime Minister, also a Justin had made the commitment to decriminalise marijuana. I realised some time ago that our decision to drink, due drugs or smoke pot were just that; our decision. No laws will make the difference one way or the other. It's our choice. The decision is the same, for abortion, prostitution or suicide. Our choice.

We don't need more laws. We have had the laws for thousands of years. We need more listening to the voice of God and obeying. If God puts that funny feeling in the pit of your stomach, recall the scriptures or say a quick prayer, but do heed His voice.

I love to watch the original NCIS TV show. In it the boss, Gibbs is always saying; "his gut is telling him". We need to get back to our gut feeling; a knowing; a discernment of what is right and wrong.

We need to go deep; be deep believers, and if you men are having trouble with the whole deep idea, just put it in football terms and here the coach yelling "go deep".

Luke 5:4
When He had stopped speaking, He said to Simon, "Launch out into the deep and let down your nets for a catch.

St. Theresa of Avila put it this way:

It's a matter of practicing the virtues, of surrendering to God in everything, of bringing our lives into harmony with whatever His Majesty arranges for us, of desiring that His will – not ours- be done.

John 14:2
"In My Father's house are many mansions; if it were not so, I would have told you. I go to prepare a place for you.

Is the Lord telling us that there are many journeys to heaven, and that the better the journey the better the accommodations in heaven? Sorry no cheap seats in heaven. Well we will find out when we get there.

Luke 7:28
"For I say to you, among those born of women, there is not a greater prophet than John the Baptist; but he who is least in the Kingdom of God is greater than he.

It's Who You Know

Have you ever heard this expression: "It's not what you know but who you know?" It does seem to be true, whether it's the job you get from the person you know to the line you move up in because you know someone in front.

What we seem to have forgotten is that we believers know the One who owns and runs the whole universe. Oh and guess what, you don't just know Him you are related to Him. Yes, you are a child of the living God, with all His rights, privileges and oh yes His inheritance.

So many live far below the standard of living that God intends for us to enjoy. God wants our journey to be blessed. Scripture declares we become a new "Creation in Christ".

2 Cor. 5:17
Therefore; if anyone is in Christ, he is a new creation; old things have passed away; behold all things have become new.

We have a new identity. It is the witness protection plan in reverse. You don't go into hiding with your new identity, nor do you not contact family and friends. No, the exact opposite should happen with your new identity. You should come out of your hiddenness and announce to everyone what God has done for you.

Young people have been increasingly distancing themselves from Church, and I can't say that I blame them. They are marrying much later, if they marry at all. I believe that the church and believers can share in the blame of it here. When is the last time you celebrated your gift to be able to attend church? When is the last time you celebrated and demonstrated your joy from being married? This new generation is looking to experience life, to experience church, to experience God. Where do they look? Movies? Internet? I'm just asking? Does not our Almighty God want us to experience Him?

Church we need to show God to the world! The people need to experience God when they come! Faith is a journey and we need to become the best tour guides we can for Him. We need to present a journey, an experience that any and every one would be excited and impatient to begin.

The Holy Spirit will be our guide. We need to leave the intellect and the philosophy behind, and let the Holy Spirit do His work on the travelers.

God desires that all His people know that it's okay to be broken, it's okay to be vulnerable, it's safe to surrender. Trust God.

John 3:18
He who believes in Him is not condemned; but he who does not believe is condemned already, because he has not believed in the name of the only begotten Son of God.

And what is the first step on our journey?

Mark 10:39
They said to Him, "We are able." So Jesus said to them, you will indeed drink the cup that I drink, and with the baptism I am baptized with you will be baptized.

There is Hope

James 1:21
Therefore lay aside all filthiness and overflow of wickedness, and receive with meekness the implanted word which is able to save your souls.

Do you have selective hearing?

Rom. 10:17
So then faith comes by hearing, and hearing by the word of God.

Now if you are saying to yourself, I don't have the time to read you are still okay. Yes, you can buy CD's and DVD's but much better than this, the Holy Spirit can and does down load scripture to your heart and your mind. There are many cases of uneducated people having scripture supernaturally down loaded. Smith-Wigglesworth who was one of the world's greatest healers and evangelist was a living case for this. He was unable to read, or write, and even had a speech stutter, but he went on to save and heal hundreds of thousands all over the world.

The word of God is God's will for all of us.

John 14:6
Jesus said to him, "I am the way, the truth, and the life. No one comes to the Father except through Me.

Are you concerned that you cannot hear from God? The mind receives head knowledge and the heart receives spirit knowledge.

John 14:24
"*God is Spirit, and those who worship Him must worship in spirit and truth.*"

I have previously said that we are called to a personal relationship with God, not religious activity, and that our belief or Faith is the trigger to calling down blessings. Our belief in Jesus Christ opens our direct line of communication to God Himself. We sing a funny song in church about Jesus on the main line and calling Him up.

If you read more than one of the Saints lives, you will see the pattern of their deep and complete dependence on going to God with everything. As I have said we need to go deeper, to live in the realm of our spirit, not our bodies.

Psalm 77:6
I call to remembrance my song in the night;

I meditate within my heart, and my spirit makes diligent search.

Jesus told us the way. He told believers to ask God to open the eyes of their heart.

Eph. 1:17,18
That the God of our Lord Jesus Christ, the Father of glory, may give to you the Spirit of wisdom and revelation in the knowledge of Him,

The eyes of your understanding being enlightened; that you may know what is the hope of His calling, what are the riches of the glory of His inheritance in the saints.

Once the eyes of your understanding are opened you will not just know of Jesus but you will truly know Him in a deep personal way.

Heb. 11:1

Now faith is the substance of things hoped for, the evidence of things not seen.

Hope

- a feeling that what is wanted will happen; desire accompanied by expectation
- the thing that one has a hope for
- a reason for hope
- a person or thing on which one may have some hope

Would you not agree that the best description of hope is Jesus?

I agree with Joyce Meyers when she says that church attendance will no more make you a Christian than sitting in your garage will make you a car. There is so much hopelessness in the world. There is an answer, an antidote, a miracle cure, and it's called Jesus.

Eph. 4:4

There is one body and one Spirit, just as you were called in one hope of your calling:

Do you have a desire as I do to help your family, your neighbour, the world? Let's give them hope; let's give them Jesus. Let's show them Jesus through our own hope. There was a movie some time ago by the name of Hope Floats. It wasn't a bad movie but the name of it really stuck with me. I believe hope does float on a river of hope carried by all of our hope in Jesus. I would like to challenge you to help get this river of hope raging till its banks overflow.

Rom. 5:5
Now hope does not disappoint, because the love of God has been poured out in our hearts by the Holy Spirit who was given to us.

Nowadays society likes to blame parents for everything, from spawning murderers to the reason for your bad grades. My own mother was physically abused by her mother but thankfully she never carried it forward. She was funny and brought a ray of sunshine to many lives. My father was placed by his parents in an orphanage at the age of 7 but that made him determined to have a successful home and family life which he still does at 92. I mention these things to make the point that we can choose how and if we will rise above our childhoods and above our circumstances. We are all capable of faith and hope and can be a light in a very dark world.

Heb. 6:19,20
This hope we have is an anchor of the soul, both sure and steadfast, and which enters the Presence behind the veil,

Where the forerunner has entered for us, even Jesus, having become High Priest forever according to the order of Melchizedek,

Someone once said: "People don't care how much you know until they know how much you care"

A very true statement. If you want to take Jesus to the world the first thing they need to know is how very, very much God loves them.

John 3:16

"For God so loved the world that He gave His only begotten Son, that whoever believes in Him should not parish but have everlasting life."

When we know how much God loves us; we will desire to please Him as His children. Perhaps there is a key to parenting here? As my son Justin says of his 2-year-old daughter Kenzie; she's like a parrot; she repeats everything. Through our daily rituals; whether it is prayer, thankfulness for our blessings, or our quiet dependence on Him, we will become an example not only to our children but to the world.

As Ghandi said:" if you want peace in the world start with your children."

Isa. 11:6

"The wolf also shall dwell with the lamb, the leopard shall lie down with the young goat, the calf and the young lion and the fatling together; and a little child shall lead them.

Journey's End

1 John 3:2
Beloved, now we are children of God; and it has not yet been revealed what we shall be, but we know that when He is revealed, we shall be like Him, for we shall see Him as He is

We are given the conclusion to make our journey perfect.

Eccl. 12: 13,14
Let us hear the conclusion of the whole matter:

Fear God and keep His commandments, for this is man's all.

For God will bring every work into judgement, including every secret thing, whether good or evil.

Writing this book has been a most rewarding journey for me, and now is the time for me to share my reward. I have written what I have heard in my spirit. I pray you will hear your Father in heaven speaking to you?

Jere. 9: 23,24
Thus says the Lord:

"Let not the wise man glory in his wisdom,

Let not the mighty man glory in his might,

Nor let the rich man glory in his riches;

But let him who glories glory in this,

That he understands and knows Me,

That I Am the Lord exercising lovingkindness, judgement, and righteousness in the earth.

For in these I delight."

Says the Lord

In summation of His message.

Matt. 25:32
"All the nations will be gathered before Him, and He will separate them one from another, as a shepherd divides his sheep from the goats.

Rev. 22:7
"Behold I Am coming quickly! Blessed is he who keeps the words of the prophecy of this book."

This book is about the journey and not the writer. If you have an issue with the message, please go to Him yourself.

The New King James version of the Bible was used and the New World Dictionary.

The Holy Bible, The New King James Version, Thomas Nelson Inc. Copyright 1992

Webster's New World Dictionary by Simon & Schuster, Inc. Copyright 1970, 1972, 1974, 1976, 1978, 1979, 1980, 1982, and 1984

www.ingramcontent.com/pod-product-compliance
Lightning Source LLC
LaVergne TN
LVHW051838080426
835512LV00018B/2951